Schöningh

[redacted]

TEACHERS' BOOK

Discover ...

SHAKESPEARE PLAYS

edited by Engelbert Thaler

William Shakespeare

Much Ado About Nothing

by Rainer Gocke and Franziska Quabeck

Sprachliche Betreuung: Joanna Becker

Acknowledgements

p. 30, 69, 70: C. Walter Hodges, 1965; p. 68 top: © BBC 2005; p. 68 bottom: © 1993 Renaissance Films PLC and The Samuel Goldwyn Company; other illustrations: Verlagsarchiv Schöningh

Every effort has been made to supply complete copyright information for the texts and pictures included here. Should such entries be incomplete or contain errors, we request copyright owners to contact the publishers so that we can proceed with the necessary corrections.

www.schoeningh-schulbuch.de
Schöningh Verlag, Jühenplatz 1–3, 33098 Paderborn

Druck 5 4 3 2 / Jahr 2014 13 12 11
Die letzte Zahl bezeichnet das Jahr dieses Druckes.

Umschlaggestaltung: Franz-Josef Domke, Hannover
Umschlagabbildung: © defd
Druck und Bindung: westermann druck GmbH, Braunschweig

ISBN 978-3-14-040119-7

Inhaltsverzeichnis

Discover ... Much Ado About Nothing

Die didaktische Konzeption

Die Themenheftreihe *Discover ... William Shakespeare* richtet sich an Schülerinnen und Schüler der Sekundarstufe II und bereitet in Anlehnung an die Einheitlichen Prüfungsanforderungen in der Abiturprüfung (EPA) und die Rahmenrichtlinien der einzelnen Bundesländer Dramen von William Shakespeare methodisch-didaktisch auf.

Der Einstieg in das Drama erfolgt über eine Doppelseite „Getting started" mit Bildmaterial und einigen Einstiegsaufgaben. Vor jeder Szene entlastet eine kurze Inhaltszusammenfassung die Lektüre. Der Dramentext steht in der Hauptspalte, während die Randspalte Annotationen, Bildmaterial (Theaterinszenierungen, Gemälde etc.), Info-Texte und gelegentlich Lesebeobachtungen (im Sinne eines „guided reading") enthält.

Im sich anschließenden Aufgabenapparat unter dem Titel „Activities" werden die Aufgaben zu thematisch zusammengehörigen Blöcken geordnet. Diese Aufgaben lassen sich den drei maßgeblichen Bereichen zuordnen: a) Inhalt (*comprehension*), b) Stil, Struktur, Intention (*analysis*), c) Evaluation, Produktion (*evaluation, creation*).

Am Ende jedes Aktes sowie am Ende des ganzen Dramas dienen rückblickende Aufgaben unter der Überschrift „Reviewing Act X" bzw. „Reviewing the play" der Zusammenfassung. Für den Unterricht nützliche Zusatzmaterialien stehen als „Con-Texts" im Anhang. Der Lehrerband enthält neben „Musterlösungen" zu allen Aufgaben zusätzliche Empfehlungen für den Unterrichtsverlauf mit möglichen Tafelbildern, mehrere Kopiervorlagen sowie eine Klausur.

Prof. Dr. Engelbert Thaler, Herausgeber

Tabellarische Textübersicht

Act, Scene	Number of Lines	Essential Features/Key quotations
1.1	274	Relatively long exposition scene; introduction of nearly all main characters, gradual filling of the stage: 1–76: Leonato, Hero, Beatrice, Messenger; 77–127: The above plus Don Pedro, Claudio, Benedick, Balthasar, Don John; 128–162: Dialogue between Claudio + Benedick: friends and soldiers; 163–234: The above plus Don Pedro (so far all in prose). 235–274: Final dialogue (in verse): Pedro + Claudio: planned stratagem leading to marriage between Claudio + Hero '… a kind of merry war betwixt Signor Benedick and her (50 f.), 'my dear Lady Disdain!' (96) '… a professed tyrant to their sex?' (134), 'Would you buy her, that you enquire after her?' (143), 'I will assume thy part in some disguise, … to her will I break' (266–271)
1.2	23	Very short prose dialogue; two elderly brothers; misinterpreted report on eavesdropping episode. '… overheard by a man of mine … the prince … loved my niece your daughter' (9 ff.)
1.3	59	1–32: Another prose dialogue, this time between two villains. 33–59: The above plus third villain; evil intentions; sombre atmosphere; counter-movement; report on another eavesdropping episode, this time correctly interpreted by villains. '… why are you thus out of measure sad?' (1 f.), '… a moral medicine to a mortifying mischief' (9 f.), '… rather a canker in a hedge, than a rose in his grace' (21), 'I am a plain-dealing villain' (25 f.), '… any model to build mischief on' (37), '… food to my displeasure' (51 f.)
2.1	332	A very long scene, nearly all in prose, except Claudio's soliloquy (147–157), full of movement, music, dancing, masks, disguise, banter, but also wickedness and villainy. Nearly a dozen changes in the stage-society, marking different phases, themes, moods. 1–69: Leonato, Antonio, Hero, Beatrice: two contrasting pairs: elderly brothers vs young heroines. Humorous family banter about getting a husband: '… thou wilt never get a husband if thou be so shrewd of thy tongue' (17 f.), 'I hope to see you one day fitted with a husband' (47 f.), '… wooing, wedding, and repenting, …' (59 ff.) 61–114: The above plus Don Pedro, Claudio, Benedick, Balthasar, Don John, Borachio, Margaret, Ursula, and others, most of them masked. The stage crowded; mutual teasing, on the whole good-natured: '… your excellent wit? Can virtue hide itself?' (102 f.), '… the prince's jester, a very dull fool' (116) 132–146: Don John, Borachio, Claudio: two villains and their victim. Claudio pretending to be Benedick, but recognised by the villains. John trying to dissuade him from marrying Hero. Evil intention, darker atmosphere: '… she is no equal for his birth' (139 f.) 147–157: Claudio solo, reflecting in verse on ill news, in a negative mood, showing how easily he can be influenced to give up his beloved Hero: '… the prince woos for himself … beauty is a witch … farewell, Hero' (149–157)
2.2	47	A relatively short prose dialogue among the two principal villains of the play, echoing scene 1.3. Somewhat surprisingly it is Borachio, the 'assistant', and not Don John, the main representative of evil, who dominates the scene and develops the nasty scheme to ruin Hero's reputation. His stratagem: a sort of 'play within the play' (see con-text), presenting false appearances including a false interpretation: '… I am sick in displeasure … How canst thou cross this marriage?' (5 ff.), 'The poison of that lies in you to temper' (18), 'Proof enough, to misuse the prince, to vex Claudio, to undo Hero, and kill Leonato' (25 f.), '… see me at her chamber window, hear me call Margaret Hero, hear Margaret term me Claudio … I will so fashion the matter …' (34 ff.) Note that Borachio presents himself as author, director and actor in his 'play within', thus resembling Shakespeare himself, who also fulfilled the same functions with regard to his own theatre.
2.3	230	A long scene, mainly in prose, except lines 32–52 and Balthasar's song (56–71), very often interpreted as one of the highlights of Shakespearean comedy in general. Balanced and elaborate structure, centering around an eavesdropping episode, which is in fact a kind of 'play within', framed by a prelude, an epilogue, two interludes and various soliloquies: 1–7: Prelude, Benedick sends his boy away and evokes the romantic setting indirect stage-direction: 'the orchard' (4)

Act, Scene	Number of Lines	Essential Features/Key quotations
		8–31: first soliloquy, containing his reflections on Claudio's turning from a soldier into a lover (8–19), his assertion that such a transformation will never happen to himself, unless the lady exhibits all the ingredients of perfection (19–30), finally his intention to hide himself in order to eavesdrop on his approaching friends (31): '... a fool ... dedicates his behaviours to love (9) ... turned orthography, his words are a fantastical banquet ... (18 f.) ... may I be so converted ... ? ... love ... shall never make me such a fool (22 ff.) ... till all graces be in one woman ... rich ... wise ... virtuous ... fair ... mild ... noble ... an angel: of good discourse, an excellent musician (25 ff.) ... I will hide me in the arbour' (30 f.) 29–80: A first interlude, containing the friends' preparations for their benevolent scheme, Balthasar's melancholic song (which, incidentally, serves as a kind of motto or prelude to Branagh's film), and Benedick's sarcastic comment on this, spoken 'aside', i. e. to himself and the audience: 'See you where Benedick hath hid himself?' (35) '... Note this before my notes, There's not a note of mine that's worth the noting.' (50 f.) (An allusion to the title of the play and a good example of an artist's affected modesty!): 'Sigh no more, ladies ... Men were deceivers ever ... constant never ... let them go ...' (56 ff.) '... And he had been a dog that would have howled thus, they would have hanged him' (76 f.) 85–193: The friends' benevolent scheme put into action, the 'play within' (see con-text), with 'aside' comments by the schemers ('actors') and the hidden Benedick ('stage-audience'). As the plotters move between critical and flattering remarks about Benedick, the latter finds himself in a kind of hot-and-cold bath. Finally the plotters decide to play a similar trick on Beatrice, thus keeping the audience in suspense and expectation for the following scene: 'Beatrice ... in love with Signor Benedick ... the fowl sits she loves him with enraged affection ... Bait the hook well, this fish will bite (86–101) ... I should think this a gull, but that the white-bearded fellow speaks it ... He hath ta'en th'infection ... my daughter tells us all (110–122) ... Then down upon her knees she falls, weeps, sobs, beats her head, tears her hair, prays, curses ... It were good that Benedick knew of it by some other ... He would make but a sport of it ... she is an excellent sweet lady ... virtuous ... exceeding wise In everything but in loving Benedick. (133–147) He is a very proper man ... a good outward happiness ... very wise ... does indeed show some sparks that are like wit ... valiant wise ... christianlike ... unworthy so good a lady ... Let there be the same net spread for her.' (163–189) 194–214: Benedick's second soliloquy: His comic conversion from pride to modesty: 'This can be no trick ... love me? ... it must be requited ... I must not seem proud ... I will be horribly in love with her ... doth not the appetite alter? ... the world must be peopled ... I do spark some marks of love in her.' 215–222: Second interlude: a short dialogue between 'converted' Benedick and 'non-converted' Beatrice: 'Against my will I am sent to bid you come in to dinner ... You take pleasure then in the message ... just so much as you may take on a knife's point.' 225–230: Epilogue: Benedick's final soliloquy: his misinterpretation of Beatrice's behaviour and his complete conversion from misogynist to romantic lover: '... there's a double meaning in that ... that's as much as to say, any pains that I take for you is as easy as thanks ... I will go get her picture.'
3.1	116	A scene of average length, all in verse, and run exclusively by female characters. It obviously parallels the preceding scene, but also contains a number of differences, thus fulfilling the aesthetic principle of repetition plus variation. 1–14: Margaret sent away by Hero to fetch Beatrice and to put her in an eavesdropping position, thus preparing the audience for another 'play within'. 15–33: Hero's instructions to Ursula, continuing the preparations for 'play within', the whole larded with satiric remarks: '... tell her ... our whole discourse / Is all of her ... there will she hide ... / To listen to our purpose ... My talk to thee must be how Benedick / Is sick in love with Beatrice ... So angle we for Beatrice, ...' (4–29) 34–103: Hero's stratagem at work. The schemers painting a rather negative picture of Beatrice, not forgetting to caricature Benedick as a pining lover who adores stone-hearted Beatrice in spite of all: '... she is too disdainful ... Disdain and scorn ride sparkling in her eyes, / Misprising what they look on ... she cannot love ... She is so self-endeared ... So turns she every man the wrong side out, ... Therefore let Benedick like covered fire / Consume away in sighs ...'(34–78) 104–106: Ursula and Hero rejoicing at the success of their plot: 'She's limed ... we have caught her ... Some Cupid kills with arrows, some with traps.' (104–106) 107–116: Beatrice's final soliloquy, showing her conversion from cold-hearted lady to ardent lover. Rhyme scheme: abab cdcd ee; cf last 10 lines of a Shakespearean sonnet: 'What fire is in mine ears? ... Benedick, love on, I will requite thee, / Taming my wild heart to thy loving hand ...' (107–112)

Act, Scene	Number of Lines	Essential Features/Key quotations
3.2	112	All in prose; clearly divided into two contrasting parts: 1–66: After the success of their stratagem (2.3) the three tricksters, Don Pedro, Claudio and Leonato, poke fun at their victim, the transformed Benedick, who now shows himself interested in fashion and is obviously not amused to be the object of scorn and derision: 'Gallants, I am not as I have been ... sadder ... in love ... tooth-ache ... everyone cannot master a grief, but he that has it ... strange disguises ... brushes his hat a-mornings ... loss of a beard ... the sweet youth's in love ... melancholy ... wash his face ... paint himself ... the two bears will not bite one another when they meet.' (12–66) 67–112: Following the exit of Benedick and Leonato and marked by the entrance of Don John, there is a remarkable change of tone and atmosphere, as the villain puts Borachio's slanderous scheme into action: 'impediment ... marriage ... suit ill-spent ... labour ill-bestowed ... the lady is disloyal ... Leonato's Hero, your Hero, every man's Hero ... you shall see ... to change your mind ... will I shame her ... disgrace her ... you are my witnesses ... let the issue show itself.' (77–108)
3.3	158	In some senses a central scene: being no. 9 out of 17 scenes it marks the middle of the play; the preceding and the following parts are also nearly equal in length, i. e. number of lines. In addition there is the first real change of place: from Leonato's house and garden to a street somewhere in Messina. Above all, with the relatively late introduction of some altogether different, farcical characters and their continual use of malapropisms there is a complete change of the stage-society, class and atmosphere. 1–91: Farcical instructions given by the head of the local police to his men: 'comprehend all vagrom men ... most tolerable and not to be endured ... be vigitant ...' (21–91) 85–158: Another eavesdropping episode: Borachio informs Conrade, both of them being Don John's villainous companions, about the success of the slanderous 'performance' at Hero's window, which took place between scenes 2.2 and 2.3. They are overheard by the forces of law and order and immediately arrested, an important turning point of the main plot: '... I have earned of Don John a thousand ducats ... I have tonight wooed Margaret ... by the name of Hero ... Claudio and my master planted, and placed, and possessed, by my master Don John, saw afar off in the orchard this amiable encounter ... the devil my master knew she was Margaret ... my villainy ... did confirm any slander that Don John had made ...' (96–139) 'We charge you in the prince's name ... we have here recovered the most dangerous piece of lechery ...' (144 ff.)
3.4	84	A transition scene: final preparations for Hero's wedding. 1–33: Hero and her waiting women discuss fashion and further ingredients of marriage: '... your other robato ... I'll wear this ... the new tire ... your gown's a most rare fashion ... night-gown ... cloth o'gold laced with silver ... my heart is exceeding heavy ...'Twill be heavier soon by the weight of a man.' (6–24) 34–84: Beatrice enters, obviously a little love-sick and not very happy about Hero getting married first. Ursula announces the arrival of the men who have come to fetch Hero to her wedding: 'I am exceeding ill, heigh ho ... For a hawk, a horse, or a husband? ... I am sick ... all the gallants of the town are come to fetch you to church. (45–83)
3.5	56	Comic scene in prose, Shakespeare using delaying technique to increase suspense and expectation in the audience waiting for the wedding and the discovery of John's plot. Leonato's eagerness to get to the wedding contrasts with the policemen's long-winded and malapropriate explanations: '... it is a busy time with me ... Comparisons are odorous ... I would fain know what you have to say ... our watch tonight ha' ta'en a couple of as arrant knaves as any in Messina ... when the age is in, the wit is out ... comprehended two aspitious persons ... to examination these men ... set down our excommunication ...' (4–55)
4.1	325	The longest and most dramatic scene in the play, mostly in verse, except lines 1–21, 140 f., 251–325. It contains elements of ritual, violent accusations, helpless distress, wise recognition of the truth, astute stratagem and finally true love. 1–28: The wedding ceremony seemingly under way, Claudio's 'No' not taken seriously: '... only to the plain form of marriage ... come hither ... to marry this lady? No ... Will you with free and unconstrained Soul / Give me this maid your daughter? ... this rich and precious gift?' (1–26) 29–150: Claudio's 'coup de théâtre', his melodramatic accusations against Hero, her helpless defense and fainting, Benedick standing apart, Beatrice defending Hero, Leonato's hyperbolical condemnation of his daughter:

Act, Scene	Number of Lines	Essential Features/Key quotations
		'... take her back again ... this rotten orange ... the sign and semblance of her honour ... how like a maid she blushes here! ... show of truth ... cunning sin cover itself ... She knows the heat of a luxurious bed ... seemed ... seeming ... seem ... intemperate in your blood ... savage sensuality ... This looks not like a nuptial ... God defend me ... I talked with no man ... Did see her, hear her ... Talk with a ruffian ... a liberal villain ... thy outward graces ... most foul, most fair (NB: Cf. Macbeth, 1.1.12 + 1.3.36: 'Fair is foul, and foul is fair ... So fair and foul a day I have not seen') ... pure impiety, and impious purity (NB: a combination of oxymora and chiasmus) ... Why how now, cousin, wherefore sink you down? ... Dead I think, help, uncle! ... Death is the fairest cover for her shame ... Why ever wast thou lovely in my eyes? ... she is fallen / Into a pit of ink, that the wide sea / Hath drops too few to wash her clean again ... I know not what to say ... Oh on my soul my cousin is belied ... Confirmed, confirmed ... let her die.' (29–150) 151–250: Friar Francis re-interprets Hero's blushing; Benedick begins to suspect Don John; the friar develops his stratagem; Benedick and Leonato agree: '... noting ... blushing apparitions ... innocent shames ... errors ... this sweet lady ... guiltless ... biting error ... misled ... The practice of it lives in John the bastard ... let my counsel sway you ... daughter ... left for dead ... secretly kept in mournful epitaphs ... rites ... burial ... Change slander to remorse ... lamented pitied and excused ... what we have we prize not to be worth ... The supposition of the lady's death, / Will quench the wonder of her infamy ... let the friar advise you ... well consented ... die to live ... have patience and endure.' (153–250) 251–325: Left alone on the stage, Benedick and Beatrice mutually reveal their love for each other, Beatrice being less enthusiastic, more careful, more demanding, complaining that – as a woman – she cannot revenge Hero herself; Benedick finally agrees to take action against Claudio: '... have you wept all this while? ... I will not desire that ... I do believe your fair cousin is wronged ... any way to show such friendship? ... I do love nothing in the world so well as you ... strange ... it were possible for me to say, I loved nothing so well as you, but believe me not ... I confess nothing, nor I deny nothing: I am sorry for my cousin ... Beatrice, thou lovest me ... I love thee ... I was about to protest I loved you ... bid me do anything for thee ... Kill Claudio ... not for the wide world ... You kill me to deny it ... Oh that I were a man ... God that I were man! I would eat his heart in the market place ... Sweet Hero, she is wronged ... slandered ... undone ... oh that I were a man ... I will die as a woman with grieving ... I am engaged, I will challenge him ...' (251–321)
4.2	71	A farcical parody of a courtroom trial, serving as 'comic relief' after the highly emotional church scene. As in the scenes 3.2 and 3.4, the forces of order are characterized by their abundant use of malapropisms and by a rather peculiar conception of legal procedures: '... our whole dissembly appeared ... exhibition to examine ... this is flat perjury, to call a prince's brother villain ... I do not like thy look ... Thou wilt be condemned to everlasting redemption ... Prince John is this morning secretly stolen away.' (1–54)
5.1	304	The second longest scene in the play, again mixing verse and prose as well as serious and comic elements. 1–107 (all in verse): Leonato's bitter complaint about his daughter's lost honour is followed by a highly aggressive encounter between the two elderly brothers against Don Pedro and Claudio: '... cease thy counsel ... give not me counsel ... Bring me a father that so loved his child ... And bid him speak of patience ... My griefs cry louder than advertisement (= advice) ... there was never yet philosopher, / That could endure the tooth-ache patiently.' (6–36) '... thou dost wrong me, thou dissembler, thou ... Thou hast so wronged mine innocent child and me / That I am forced to ... challenge thee to trial of a man ... thou hast belied mine innocent child ... she lies buried with her ancestors ... framed by thy villainy ... Thou hast killed my child ... she is dead, slandered to death by villains ... Boys, apes, braggarts, Jacks, milksops' (53–90) 110–188 (in prose): The exit of the two brothers is followed by the entrance of Benedick, also in a highly aggressive mood and willing to challenge Claudio to a duel, as promised to Beatrice in 4.1. Whereas Claudio and Don Pedro first ignore his intention and try to continue their usual banter, Benedick insists on fighting Claudio and formally ends his friendship with Don Pedro: '... We had like to have had our two noses snapped off with two old men without teeth ... wilt thou use thy wit? ... It is in my scabbard ... You are a villain ... Beatrice praised thy wit the other day ... Fare you well, boy, you know my mind ... my lord, I must discontinue your company: your brother the bastard is fled from Messina: you have ... killed a sweet and innocent lady ... (112–175) 178–234 (mainly in prose, except lines 221–228): After Benedick's exit and Claudio's and Don Pedro's comments on the seriousness of the situation, the newly arrived policemen and their prisoners bring about yet another change of mood and an important step forward towards the solution of the main plot:

Act, Scene	Number of Lines	Essential Features/Key quotations
		'He is in earnest ... In most profound earnest ... hath challenged thee? ... Most sincerely ... How now, two of my brother's men bound? ... what offence have these men done? ... they have committed false report ... secondarily, they are slanders, sixth and lastly, they have belied a lady, thirdly they have verified unjust things ... This learned constable is too cunning to be understood ... what your wisdoms could not discover, these shallow fools have brought to light ... your brother incensed me to slander the Lady Hero ... the lady is dead upon mine and my master's false accusation ... Sweet Hero, now thy image does appear / In the rare semblance that I loved it first.' (178–228) 235–279: The re-appearance of Leonato and Antonio, accompanied with the Sexton who was in charge of the courtroom trial (4.2), is followed by a formal verse dialogue, in which Borachio confirms his guilt, Claudio and Don Pedro repent their error and offer to accept any punishment, whereas Leonato develops yet another stratagem to unite Claudio and Hero after all: 'Which is the villain? ... look on me ... Art thou the slave that with thy breath hast killed / Mine innocent child? ... Yea, even I alone ... choose your revenge yourself ... yet sinned I not, / But in mistaking ... to satisfy this good old man, / I would bend under any heavy weight ... my brother hath a daughter, / Almost a copy of my child that's dead ... Give her the right you should have given her cousin, / And so dies my revenge.' (235–268) 280–304: The concluding prose dialogue is again dominated by Dogberry's usual distortion of thought and language and leads to a gradual clearing of the stage: 'God keep your worship ... I humbly give you leave to depart, and if a merry meeting may be wished, God prohibit it ...' (296–298)
5.2	86	A prose scene (except Benedick's attempted song [21–25]), mainly dominated by banter, Benedick being the only character who remains on stage throughout. 1–35: Benedick's playful conversation with Margaret, containing a number of sexual allusions, is followed by his last soliloquy, in which he modestly confesses his inability to declare his love poetically: '... Will you then write me a sonnet in praise of my beauty? ... no man over me, why, shall always keep below ... Thy wit is as quick as the greyhound's mouth ... And yours, as blunt as the fencer's foils ...' (3–11) '... love ... I cannot show it in rhyme ... no rhyme to lady but baby ... scorn horn ... school fool ... I cannot woo in festival terms.' (31–35) 36–79: After Beatrice's inquiry about Benedick's promised duel with Claudio follows a curiously detached conversation, in which both partners try not to commit themselves more than necessary: '... what hath passed between you and Claudio ... Claudio undergoes my challenge ... for which of my good parts did you first suffer love for me? ... I do suffer love indeed, for I love thee against my will ... Thou and I are too wise to woo peaceably.' (40–61) 80–86: When Ursula brings in good news, the long-awaited happy ending seems near. Benedick reacts with a poetic outburst, but does not forget to debunk it in the end: '... it is proved my Lady Hero hath been falsely accused, the prince and Claudio mightily abused, and Don John is the author of it all, who is fled and gone ... I will live in thy heart, die in thy lap and be buried in thy eyes: and moreover, I will go with thee to thy uncle's (81–86)
5.3	33	A rather strange mourning ceremony, all in rhymed verse, with varying rhyming schemes. As we are in a comedy and aware that no one has 'really' died, the scene may appear as a parody: 'Done to death by slanderous tongues, Was the Hero that here lies: ... Give her fame which never dies ...' (3–6)
5.4	122	The final scene, uniting Claudio and Hero as well as Benedick and Beatrice and bringing everything – at least on the surface – to a happy ending. 1–51: Leonato prepares for the final stratagem, asking all the ladies to mask themselves. Left alone with the friar and Leonato, Benedick asks Leonato for Beatrice's hand in marriage, which is granted. After Don Pedro's and Claudio's arrival, the atmosphere seems still strained. Claudio promises to marry any lady that he will be asked to. Love does not seem to play a part. 'Withdraw into a chamber by yourselves, / And when I send for you come hither masked ... brother, / You must be father to your brother's daughter.' (11–15) '... My will is ... this day to be conjoined, / In the state of honourable marriage ...'(28–30) 'Claudio ... are you determined, / Today to marry with my brother's daughter? ... I hold my mind were she an Ethiop.' (35–38) '... Benedick ... you have such a February face, / So full of frost, of storm, and cloudiness?' (40–42)

Act, Scene	Number of Lines	Essential Features/Key quotations
		52–96: The ladies re-enter masked; after the wedding-ceremony Hero drops her mask and is only then recognised by her husband. Benedick, on the other hand, asks Beatrice to reveal her identity before marriage. Both of them continue their 'merry war' for a while, pretending not to love each other, until they are confronted with former declarations of love which they cannot deny: 'Which is the lady I must seize upon? ... let me see your face ... not, till you take her hand, / Before this friar, and swear to marry her ... I am your husband ... Another Hero? ... She died ... but whiles her slander lived' (53–66) '... which is Beatrice? ... Do not you love me? ... no more than reason (2x) ... They swore that you were almost sick for me ... They swore that you were willnigh dead for me ... then you do not love me? ... No truly, but in friendly recompense ... here's a paper written in his hand, / A halting sonnet of his own poor brain ... And here's another Writ in my cousin's hand, / Containing her affection unto Benedick' (72–90) 91–122: After 90 lines in verse, the comedy concludes in prose. Benedick sums up his philosophy, suggests general reconciliation, recommends marriage to the prince, and upon the news that the villain of the piece has been taken in flight, postpones his punishment. The play ends in music and dancing, symbols of peace and harmony: '... man is a giddy thing ... Come, come, we are friends, let's have a dance ... that we may lighten our own hearts, and our wives' heels ... Prince, thou art sad, get thee a wife, get thee a wife ...' (104–117)

Einteilung der Aufgaben

Falls die Aufgaben nicht sukzessive bearbeitet werden sollen, kann auch eine ökonomische Einteilung anhand von thematischen Aspekten vorgenommen werden:

Thema	Aufgaben
Shakespeare und seine Zeit	Getting started – Aufgabe 1 Worksheet No. 1 Worksheet No. 4 Con-Text 'Queen Elizabeth I' – Aufgabe 4
Figurenkonstellationen/ Gesamtzusammenhang	1. 1 – Aufgabe 1 2.1 – Aufgabe 5 2.1 – Aufgabe 7 2.3 – Aufgabe 4 Reviewing Act 2 – Aufgabe 1 Reviewing Act 2 – Aufgabe 6 Reviewing Act 2 – Aufgabe 7 Reviewing Act 2 – Aufgabe 8 3.1 – Aufgabe 1 3.4 – Aufgabe 1 Reviewing Act 3 – Aufgabe 1 Reviewing Act 3 – Aufgabe 2 Reviewing Act 4 – Aufgabe 6 Reviewing Act 4 – Aufgabe 8 5.2 – Aufgabe 2 5.3 – Aufgabe 2 5.4 – Aufgabe 1 5.4 – Aufgabe 2 Reviewing Act 5 – Aufgabe 2 Reviewing the Play – Aufgabe 5 Reviewing the Play – Aufgabe 6 Reviewing the Play – Aufgabe 9 Worksheet No. 2 Worksheet No. 3 Worksheet No. 5 Worksheet No. 9
Beatrice	3.1 – Aufgabe 3 Reviewing Act 3 – Aufgabe 8 4.1 – Aufgabe 5 4.1 – Aufgabe 6 Reviewing Act 4 – Aufgabe 10 Reviewing Act 4 – Aufgabe 11 5.2 – Aufgabe 2 5.2 – Aufgabe 3 Reviewing the Play – Aufgabe 4 Con-Text 'Queen Elizabeth I' – Aufgabe 2
Benedick	2.1 – Aufgabe 3 2.1 – Aufgabe 4 2.3 – Aufgabe 1 2.3 – Aufgabe 3 2.3 – Aufgabe 5 Reviewing Act 2 – Aufgabe 5 3.2 – Aufgabe 1 Reviewing Act 3 – Aufgabe 7 Reviewing Act 3 – Aufgabe 8 5.2 – Aufgabe 2 5.3 – Aufgabe 3

Thema	Aufgaben
Claudio	2.1 – Aufgabe 2 2.1 – Aufgabe 2 2.1 – Aufgabe 3 3.2 – Aufgabe 2 Reviewing Act 3 – Aufgabe 7 4.1 – Aufgabe 2 Reviewing Act 4 – Aufgabe 4 5.1 – Aufgabe 4 5.1 – Aufgabe 5 5.1 – Aufgabe 6
Hero	2.1 – Aufgabe 6 Reviewing Act 3 – Aufgabe 3 Con-Text 'Queen Elizabeth I' – Aufgabe 1
Don John	1.3 – Aufgabe 1 – Aufgabe 2 2.2 – Aufgabe 2
Don Leonato	1.2 – Aufgabe 1 – Aufgabe 2 4.1 – Aufgabe 3 5.1 – Aufgabe 1 5.1 – Aufgabe 2
Inhaltliche Themen	
Appearance vs reality	2.1 – Aufgabe 1 Reviewing Act 2 – Aufgabe 3 Reviewing Act 2 – Aufgabe 4 Reviewing Act 3 – Aufgabe 4 Reviewing Act 3 – Aufgabe 5 4.1 – Aufgabe 4 Reviewing Act 4 – Aufgabe 5 Reviewing Act 4 – Aufgabe 7 Reviewing Act 5 – Aufgabe 1 Reviewing the Play – Aufgabe 2 Reviewing the Play – Aufgabe 7 Con-Text 'Play Within the Play' – Aufgabe 1
Gender-Stereotypen	1.1 – Aufgabe 4 Reviewing Act 4 – Aufgabe 9 5.2 – Aufgabe 2
Liebe und Heirat	1.1 Aufgabe 5 Reviewing Act 1 – Aufgabe 3 5.2 – Aufgabe 1 5.2 – Aufgabe 2 5.2 – Aufgabe 3 5.4 – Aufgabe 3 5.4 – Aufgabe 4 5.4 – Aufgabe 5 5.4 – Aufgabe 6 Reviewing Act 5 – Aufgabe 4 Reviewing the Play – Aufgabe 3 Reviewing the Play – Aufgabe 8
Intertextuelle Bezüge	Reviewing Act 1 – Aufgabe 5 2.2 – Aufgabe 3 Reviewing the Play – Aufgabe 12 Con-Text 'Play Within the Play' – Aufgabe 1 a Con-Text 'Play Within the Play' – Aufgabe 1 b Con-Text 'Queen Elizabeth I' – Aufgabe 3

Thema	Aufgaben
Formale Themen	
Komische Elemente	Reviewing Act 2 – Aufgabe 9 3.3 – Aufgabe 1 3.3 – Aufgabe 2 Reviewing Act 3 – Aufgabe 6 4.2 – Aufgabe 1 4.2 – Aufgabe 2 Reviewing the Play – Aufgabe 2 Con-Text *'Much Ado About Nothing as a Shakespearean Comedy'* – Aufgabe 1 Con-Text *'Much Ado About Nothing as a Shakespearean Comedy'* – Aufgabe 2
Genre	Reviewing Act 1 – Aufgabe 1 – Aufgabe 2 4.1 – Aufgabe 1 Reviewing Act 4 – Aufgabe 3
Struktur des Dramas	Getting Started – Aufgabe 2 – Aufgabe 3 – Aufgabe 4 1.2 – Aufgabe 3 2.2 – Aufgabe 1 Reviewing Act 2 – Aufgabe 2 3.5 – Aufgabe 1 4.1 – Aufgabe 5 5.3 – Aufgabe 1 Reviewing the Play – Aufgabe 2
Sprache	1.1 – Aufgabe 2 1.1 – Aufgabe 3 4.1 – Aufgabe 7 Reviewing the Play – Aufgabe 11
Aktualisierung des Dramas	Reviewing Act 1 – Aufgabe 5 Reviewing Act 1 – Aufgabe 7 2.3 – Aufgabe 2 2.3 – Aufgabe 6 3.1 – Aufgabe 2 3.2 – Aufgabe 3 3.3 – Aufgabe 3 4.2 – Aufgabe 3 Reviewing Act 4 – Aufgabe 10 5.3 – Aufgabe 3 Reviewing Act 5 – Aufgabe 3
ADO verfilmt (klassisch und modern)	3.4 – Aufgabe 2 Reviewing Act 4 – Aufgabe 2 Reviewing the Play – Aufgabe 10
Schülermeinung	Reviewing Act 1 – Aufgabe 4 5.1 – Aufgabe 3 Reviewing the Play – Aufgabe 1 Con-Text 'Queen Elizabeth I' – Aufgabe 4

Getting started

Die ersten Aufgaben sollten langsam an das Drama heranführen. Die erste Aufgabe ist vor allen Dingen dazu geeignet, den Schülern das Genre nahezubringen und den vorliegenden Text mehr als Theaterstück denn als „Buch“ wahrzunehmen. Aufgaben 2–4 verschaffen einen ersten Eindruck der Figurenkonstellation und der allgemeinen Thematik. An dieser Stelle kann es sehr hilfreich sein, mit einem Filmausschnitt zu arbeiten, um den Schülern die Geschwindigkeit und die Komik der Dialoge zu vermitteln, da diese Elemente beim ersten Lesen meist verborgen bleiben und der Text als solcher somit zu abstrakt erscheint. Um den Schülern die genaue Struktur der *stage society* nahezubringen, eignet sich vor allen Dingen das Diagramm der *dramatis personae*.

1. **Think of different methods a playwright might use to keep his audience on the alert. Take examples of your own experience from watching films, TV-productions, theatre performances.**
   In comedy especially, the first scene must have a certain speed to it in order to keep the audience interested and excited. Several changes in the stage society like exits and entrances contribute to a dynamic atmosphere. The introduction of numerous new characters requires the audience's focused attention in order to understand the relations etc.

2. **What information do we get about the antecedents*?**
   Don Pedro and his soldiers have been fighting a war with his estranged half-brother Don John but now the final battle is over and the brothers are reconciled. Although none of the men who come to Don Leonato's house originally come from Messina, they seem to have known Don Leonato for quite some time and he and Don Pedro are close friends. Beatrice and Benedick seem well acquainted with each other, although it is not yet clear *how* well. They have established a reputation for the 'merry war' that is going on between them, but the conflict seems to be rather a lighthearted than a grave one. Claudio noticed Hero already before he went into battle with Don Pedro but only now shows a serious design towards her.

3. **What do we learn about the characters and their relationships towards one another?**
   There is the patriarchal household on the one hand and the hierarchically structured group of soldiers on the other. The diagram of the stage society structures the *dramatis personae* hierarchically and should be consulted at this point. We know now that 1. Don Leonato and Don Pedro are friends. 2. Hero is Leonato's daughter, Beatrice his niece, and the two cousins seem very close. 3. Benedick and Claudio are close friends and obviously confide in one another. Claudio has fallen in love with Hero and Beatrice and Benedick have some sort of relationship, the particulars of which are not entirely clear yet. Don Pedro seems to be something of a father figure for Claudio. His brother Don John is included in the party but seems reluctant to play an active part in it.

4. **What techniques of information are used?**
   In order to announce the impending arrival of Don Pedro, Shakespeare has Leonato first read a letter and then question the Messenger about the particulars of the battle, which presents the opportunity of providing background information. It should be noted at this point that this is secondary information, the unreliability of which is a recurring theme in the comedy. Leonato's dialogue with the Messenger opens the

conversation to Beatrice, who inquires after Benedick, and the fact that the Messenger is unaware of their particular relationship makes it necessary for Leonato to explain, which is a method to inform the audience about the antecedents at the same time. Claudio's and Benedick's dialogue about the two girls gives us a very precise description of what an actress playing Hero should look like and Benedick's statements about her in comparison to Beatrice also suggest that Beatrice is a very attractive woman in his eyes.

Worksheet 1

How much do you know about William Shakespeare?

Try to fill in the gaps.

When did he live?	
What is the name of that historical period?	
Where was he born and where did he move later on in his life?	
What was his occupation?	
Name some of his most famous works.	
What was the name of his workplace?	
How are his works usually categorised?	
What is his standard verse form?	
Find a famous quotation from one of his works.	

Worksheet 1 Solution

✓ class test prep.

How much do you know about William Shakespeare?

When did he live?	1564–1616
What is the name of that historical period?	Elizabethan Age Renaissance
Where was he born and where did he move later on in his life?	Stratford-upon-Avon London
What was his occupation?	playwright poet actor
Name some of his most famous works.	*Macbeth, Hamlet, Romeo and Juliet, A Midsummer Night's Dream*
What was the name of his workplace?	Globe Theatre
How are his works usually categorised?	comedies tragedies histories
What is his standard verse form?	blank verse in iambic pentameter
Find a famous quotation from one of his works.	'All the world's a stage, and all the men and women merely players: they have their exits and their entrances; and one man in his time plays many parts …' *As You Like It* 2.7.139–142

Unterrichtsempfehlungen

Einstiegsmöglichkeiten in die Lektüre eines Shakespeare-Dramas erscheinen von nahezu ähnlich unerschöpflicher Vielfalt wie die vielgerühmte „infinite variety“ des Barden selbst. Vorkenntnisse des Kurses auf literarischen Gebieten, eventuell in geisteswissenschaftlichen Nachbarfächern erworben, Theaterspielpläne der Region, Einbeziehung von Probenbesuchen, Diskussionsmöglichkeiten mit Dramaturgen, Regisseuren, Schauspielern, Medienausstattung der Schule, keineswegs zuletzt persönliche Vorlieben der Kursleitung stellen eine kleine Auswahl der ungezählten Faktoren dar.
Nach wie vor ungeklärte Fragen der Autorenschaft, biographische Trivialitäten usw. sind schnellstmöglich zu erledigen durch Hinweise auf Google, Wikipedia etc. Hier eignet sich Worksheet No. 1, am besten als Hausaufgabe noch vor der ersten Sitzung der Unterrichtsreihe. Am besten geeignet als eigentlicher Einstieg in die Thematik ist oft eine Einführung in die Gattung Drama. Schülerreferate über die erwähnten Aspekte, wie auch über die shakespeareschen Sub-Gattungen *Tragedy, History, Comedy* haben sich in der Vergangenheit bewährt.
Allgemeines Brainstorming könnte mit Fragen nach Vorkenntnissen über Dramen eröffnet werden und bald um die Frage kreisen, warum Shakespeare seit Jahrhunderten der meistgespielte Dramatiker der Weltliteratur ist, zunächst auf Bühnen, dann auch im Film und Fernsehen, in jüngster Zeit immer leichter und auch preisgünstiger verfügbar auf Bild- und Tonträgern, augenblicklich vorwiegend auf DVD.
Mögliche Antworten sind wiederum vielfältig, etwa: spannende Handlungsverläufe, Unterhaltungswert, Charakterisierungskunst, Einblick in Verhaltensweisen in unterschiedlichsten Situationen, Vermittlung von „Lebensweisheit“, Faszination des Klangs, Evokationskraft der Bildersprache, Wortspiele usw.
Durchaus motivierend erscheint im Anschluss an solches Brainstorming eine mediale Präsentation des gesamten Stücks, wobei gerade im Fall von *Much Ado About Nothing* drei DVD-Versionen verfügbar sind, auf die in *Discover ... ADO* verschiedentlich Bezug genommen wird, unterstützt durch zahlreiche Illustrationen im Textheft dieser Ausgabe.
Als Klassiker gelten dabei die BBC-Version von 1984 und der Branagh-Film von 1993. Im Rahmen des BBC-TV-Shakespeare wurden von 1978–1984 sämtliche Shakespeare-Dramen produziert und in den Folgejahren weltweit mit überragendem Erfolg ausgestrahlt. Werktreue, traditionelle Kostüme und meist hochrenommierte Schauspieler der Royal Shakespeare Company (RSC) charakterisieren diese Reihe und insbesondere die gegen Ende produzierte ADO-Version.
Neun Jahre jünger ist der in der Toscana entstandene Branagh-Film von 1993 mit dem seinerzeitigen Medien-Traumpaar Kenneth Branagh und seiner damaligen Gattin Emma Thompson als Benedick und Beatrice.
Wesentlich weiter vom Original als diese Versionen entfernt sich die ebenfalls von der BBC 2005 erstellte Adaptation in der Reihe *Shakespeare Retold*. Hier wird die Handlung in die Gegenwart verlagert. Benedick und Beatrice erscheinen als TV-Moderatorenpaar, welches sich bei der Nachrichtenpräsentation neutral verhält, bei abgeschalteter Kamera jedoch unverzüglich in seinen mehr oder weniger „merry“ zu nennenden Geschlechterkrieg verfällt. Jede der skizzierten Versionen findet ihre Befürworter und Kritiker.

Grundsätzliche Einwände gegen eine antizipierte Gesamtpräsentation vor der detaillierten Lektüre liegen z. B. in der Kritik an einer spannungszerstörenden Vorwegnahme der Handlungslösung oder zu starker Fixierung der Schüler auf eine bestimmte Interpretation.
Gegenargumente: Eine Kenntnis der gesamten Komödie erleichtert die Konzentration auf wichtige Details und damit den rhythmischen Wechsel zwischen kursorischer und statarischer Lektüre. Ein übergeordnetes Lernziel erscheint geeignet, den zweiten erwähnten Einwand zu entkräften: Den Schülern sollte bewusst sein, dass jegliche Interpretation, ob bezogen auf Text, Theater, Film oder TV, gewöhnlich eine unter einer Vielzahl möglicher Deutungen ist.
Auch lässt sich alternativ über eine partielle Präsentation der jeweils zu behandelnden Textpassage nachdenken, wobei eventuell unterschiedliche Versionen miteinander verglichen werden.
Inhaltlich steht bei der Interpretation des 1. Aktes die Exposition im Vordergrund, d. h. im Fall von ADO die Präsentation fast aller wichtigen Figuren, ihr Verhältnis zueinander (hier eignen sich besonders Worksheets No. 2 und No. 3 zur Verdeutlichung), die gesellschaftliche Situation – hochgestellte Müßiggänger, erfolgreiche Soldaten nach siegreicher Schlacht – das jeweils andere Geschlecht, heiteres Gesprächsklima, aber auch ein missgünstiger, gesellschaftlich benachteiligter Außenseiter, der mit seinen Komplizen für Spannung und „Sand im Getriebe" sorgt. Frühzeitig spielt auch die leitmotivische Schein-Sein-Thematik eine Rolle, etwa in der Figur des Don John, vorgeblich dankbar und versöhnt, in Wirklichkeit Böses planend, daneben die falsch interpretierte erste Lausch-Episode (1.2). In der Anfangsphase eines Dramas verdienen ferner Strategien der Informationsvermittlung besondere Beachtung, etwa der Botenbericht oder Streitgespräche, in denen sich die Kombattanten gegenseitig Charaktereigenschaften und Begebenheiten der Vorgeschichte vorwerfen.
Generell lässt sich auch die von Shakespeare immer wieder eingesetzte Technik verschiedener Kontraste thematisieren, etwa: Große vs kleine Bühnengesellschaft (1.1 vs 1.2 + 1.3), allmählicher Auf- und Abbau der Bühnengesellschaft (1.1), Prosa vs Blankvers, alt vs jung, männlich vs weiblich, heiter vs bösartig.
Besonders wichtig sind selbstverständlich sprachliche Aspekte in Shakespeares Frühneuenglisch (keineswegs das von Schülern und anderen gern beschworene „Altenglisch"!), Wortreichtum, Bildersprache, „repartee" und andere rhetorische Figuren.
Zu warnen ist freilich davor, alles auf einmal thematisieren zu wollen. Die Schwerpunktbildung liegt glücklicherweise im pflichtgemäßen Ermessen des lehrenden Individuums. Insofern versteht sich die Gesamtheit der „activities" im Textheft nebst Lösungsvorschlägen im Teachers' Book als Angebot und Einladung zur freien Auswahl. Die Autoren hoffen auf rege Wahlbeteiligung.

Act 1 Scene 1

Solutions

Activities p. 15

1. **Look at the diagram of the stage society. What are your first impressions of the characters in the opening scene? Who do you identify as the most important characters and what are their positions in the stage society?**
The diagram clearly represents the play to be male-dominated. Apart from the fact that there are only four women out of a total of 13 people, the structure according to the characters' ranks shows that they are rather inferior. Although Beatrice is easily identifiable as one of the play's protagonists (witty, outstanding), she maintains a somewhat isolated position in this society. Her relation to Leonato as his niece includes her in the family but makes her inferior to Hero as Leonato's daughter. Since she has no family aside from Leonato and Hero and no other relation, her status as his niece is her only connection to the rest of the characters. Moreover, the grouping of female characters only on the side of the Messinian household emphasises the male domination. This should be pointed out again, when most of the foreign male characters *and* her father turn against her on the charge of adultery. This constellation isolates and at the same time unites the women in the play even more. Furthermore, the patriarchal structure emphasises Beatrice's wit, independence and unwillingness to obey rules.

2. **Look up the term 'repartee' in the glossary and find five examples in scene 1.1. What are their overall effects?**
Repartee: 'An expression taken from fencing, where it means 'counter-attack', in a comic dialogue a witty reply, often taking up a phrase used by an opponent, but giving it a different sense or even reverting the speaker's intention.

Beatrice	Benedick	Beatrice
	'My dear Lady Disdain! Are you yet living?' (96)	'Is it possible Disdain should die, while she hath such meet food to feed it as Signor Benedick?' (97/98)
'Courtesy itself must convert to Disdain, if you come in her presence.' (98/99)	'Then is Courtesy a turncoat ...' (100)	
	'... some gentleman or other shall scape a predestinate scratched face.' (107/108)	'Scratching could not make it worse, and 'twere such a face as yours were.' (109/110)
	'... you are a rare parrot-teacher.' (111)	'A bird of my tongue is better than a beast of yours.' (112)
	'I would my horse had the speed of your tongue ...' (113)	'You always end with a jade's trick ...' (116)

First of all, the remarks are witty and funny, creating a playful atmosphere, thus introducing the play as a comedy. Secondly, the continued exchange between Beatrice and Benedick singles them out as a couple. The attention focuses on their relationship, although at this point it is not quite clear whether they like or dislike each other. The question arises whether their dialogue is motivated by flirtatious banter or is grounded in a profound dislike of each other. This question will have to be kept in mind throughout the play. Thirdly, Beatrice's many repartees single her out as a very dominant character, which emphasises her cousin's passiveness and silence. Clearly, she tries to meet the men on the same level without subordinating herself, quite the contrary.

3. **'You must not, sir, mistake my niece: there is a kind of merry war betwixt Signor Benedick and her ...' Consult the glossary to find out which rhetorical device is used here. What does this mean concerning the relationship between Beatrice and Benedick?**
'Merry war' is an oxymoron. An oxymoron is a figure of speech that combines two contradictory terms. Other examples are 'deafening silence', 'bittersweet', 'sweet sorrow'. The use of an oxymoron here implies the two-sided relationship Beatrice and Benedick have or seem to have and it emphasises the fact that it is not easy to define whether this is a friendly or hostile exchange. 'Merry' indicates that they both enjoy it, they are in rather high spirits when they engage in it, and that the things they say are not meant seriously. They mock each other and do not take offence at what the other person says. However, the term 'war' at the same time implies that there is a conflict between them, which cannot be resolved peacefully. It suggests that their repartees are structured into attack and defence and it is not entirely impossible to hurt the other. They are opponents and the image of war immediately suggests that they can either win or lose. Come back to this question when they finally get married: has either of them won or lost? Have both of them won or lost?

4. **Take a closer look at the dialogue between Claudio and Benedick: How do they talk about Hero and Beatrice? What do they say about women and marriage in general? Find significant quotations from the text.**
Activities p. 16
Claudio: 'modest young lady' (131); 'Can the world buy such a jewel?' (144); 'the sweetest lady' (149); 'That I love her, I feel' (184).
Upon seeing her he is immediately enchanted and does not hesitate to declare himself in love. Since we know that he is rather young (see ll. 11–12: 'He hath borne himself beyond the promise of his age doing in the figure of a lamb the feats of a lion.'), this is not surprising but seems naïve and ridicules Romantic feelings, especially in contrast to Benedick's ironic and almost disdainful remarks.
Benedick: 'I noted her not' (130); 'professed tyrant to their sex' (134); '... she's too low for a high praise, too brown for a fair praise and too little for a great praise ... were she other than she is, she were unhandsome; and being no other than she is, I do not like her.'; 'There's her cousin, an she were not possessed with a fury, exceeds her as much in beauty as the first of May doth the last of December.' (152–154)
His rather unflattering description of Hero on the one hand presents him as cynical and unromantic, but his appreciation of Beatrice's beauty on the other hand suggests that first, Claudio might truly be exaggerating Hero's qualities and second, that Benedick is not as hostile towards Beatrice as it might seem.
While Claudio worships the woman maybe a little too much, Benedick's remarks towards her are somewhat deprecatory ('Would you buy her ... ?' 143). His negative attitude towards Claudio's confession of love also has something to do with his aversion to marriage: '... I hope you have no intent to turn husband ...' (154 f.); '... hath not the world one man, but he will wear his cap with suspicion? ... thou wilt needs thrust thy neck into a yoke, wear the print of it, and sigh away Sundays.' (158–162) Marriage is represented as a burden for men and he implies that women are fickle and not trustworthy. He seems to say that a man who marries exposes himself to the possibility of being a cuckold and loses respect and authority. It is indeed noteworthy that none of the other male characters are in fact married (even Leonato, who was married once before, playfully questions his wife's faithfulness by saying: 'Her mother hath many times told me so.' (86) Apart from the question why she had to tell him many times, the emphasis lies on the fact that he only has her word for it). The attitudes on

more than only on Benedick's side seem to be suspicious, anti-marriage, and, at times, even misogynistic, although Leonato's statement incidentally echoes a standard joke in Shakespeare, e.g.: *King Lear*, 1.1.8f.; *The Tempest*, 1.2.55ff.; *The Taming of the Shrew*, 5.2.29f. The repetition of this joke illustrates the theme of male fear of female unfaithfulness, which is repeated several times in ADO.

5. **Consult the Internet on 'arranged marriages' in different societies. What part does this social phenomenon play in your text?**
   Individual answers

6. **Imagine the actors playing Beatrice and Benedick – how would they move on stage, which gestures do you imagine them to make? Try to act out part of the dialogue (1.1.94 – 116).**
   Free activity

Act 1 Scene 2

Solutions

Activities p. 17

1. **Describe how Leonato and Antonio talk about the possible marriage.**
   Leonato wants to hold the news of Don Pedro's supposed wish to marry Hero 'as a dream till it appear itself' (17). Clearly, he rejoices at the thought of uniting his daughter to the Prince of Aragon.

2. **'that she may be better prepared for an answer' – What answer will she give? And what role does Leonato play in this?**
   The way Leonato talks about delivering the news to Hero suggests that this is not a matter of choice for her. The patriarchal dominance becomes obvious once more. Neither Leonato nor Antonio seem to be in any doubt whether she will give the answer they want her to.

Act 1 Scene 3

Solutions

Activities p. 19

1. **What kind of character is Don John?**
   As other notorious villains in Shakespeare, Don John seems to be driven by a feeling of revenge against his fate. He is referred to as a 'bastard', i.e. an illegitimate child, born without marriage, which used to be an extremely problematic position. So-called bastards were despised by society and considered to possess a bad character. As a reaction they tended to take their revenge on society. Modern psychologists might describe this as a frustration-aggression-mechanism. Similar villains in Shakespeare are Edmund in *King Lear* (also a 'bastard'), Richard of Gloucester in *Richard III* (who is physically handicapped) or Iago in *Othello*, who feels unjustly treated by his superior, Othello.
   It is quite extraordinary that such a villain occurs in a comedy. Already in his very first remark '... I am not of many words' (1.1.125) Don John appears as an outsider, if not a misfit, in the talkative society of Messina. He describes himself as a plain-dealing villain' (25). He is looking for mischief he can create and from his determination one can tell that he will succeed in one way or another. It should be kept in mind here that he claims to be unable to hide what he is, although later on he does exactly that.

2. **Why is there a conflict between Don John and Claudio?**
   Don John is jealous of Claudio because he is Don Pedro's chosen companion. He fears that Claudio will reap all the benefits that Don John believes himself to deserve as Don Pedro's brother. His repeated references to himself as a dog ('muzzle ... clog ... bite') emphasise the negative conception of his status as bastard, which is probably not the last reason why Don Pedro prefers Claudio to him and he knows that.

3. **In scene 1.3 there is another report on an eavesdropping episode. What do the reports in 1.2 and 1.3 have in common? Are there any differences?**
   Antonio's report is based on a complete misunderstanding, which might amuse the audience. We tend to feel superior to Antonio. The feeling of superiority is a basic element of comedy in general. Borachio's report (1.3.34 ff.) is right on the whole. Villains are often more intelligent than good-natured characters in Shakespeare. Yet they also make their mistakes. Borachio e.g. overlooks that Don Pedro will woo in disguise. The theme of disguise, which is linked to error, misunderstanding, false identity etc., is another characteristic feature of comedy in general and of ADO in particular.

Reviewing Act One

Solutions

Activities p. 20

1. **All of Shakespeare's works were originally divided into three different genres. Find out which ones.**
   Comedies, tragedies, histories.

2. **After the impression you got from reading act 1, would you classify ADO as a comedy and, if so, why? Are there any aspects that you find unsuitable as comic elements?**
   The first scene is funny, mainly due to the dialogue between Beatrice and Benedick. There are many puns, repartees and metaphors, which create a light and playful atmosphere. In scene 2 the typical misunderstanding and the eavesdropping alluded to also point towards a comic plot; but in scene 3 the atmosphere changes. The introduction of Don John as a serious villain, who is determined to create mischief without any reason, darkens the mood and it is still possible for him to create a tragic outcome. Which of the two possible plots will take over remains to be seen.

3. **Traditionally, Shakespearean comedies end in one or several marriages. Can you guess who will get married at the end of ADO? Find hints in the text to prove your theory.**
   Since Claudio is so elaborate about his feelings for Hero, it seems very likely that they will get married ('Can the world buy such a jewel?', '... she is the sweetest lady that ever I looked on' 144, 149), especially because he does not hesitate to take action towards this in asking Don Pedro to woo her for him. The fact that he is still very young and refers to the fact that his behaviour might seem a little hasty himself ('But lest my liking might too sudden seem, I would have salved it with a longer treatise.' 259/260), could imply that there will be some obstacles the couple will have to overcome. He does claim, however, that his affection is not entirely new but was already felt when he saw her before, which makes it seem a little stronger and less random ('But now I am returned, and that war-thoughts/Have left their places vacant, in their rooms/Come thronging soft and delicate desires,/All prompting me how fair young Hero is,/Saying I liked her ere I went to wars.' 246–250) Moreover, the fact that Don Pedro takes him entirely seriously and not only approves of the match

('That I love her, I feel.' – 'That she is worthy, I know.' 184/185), but also immediately makes plans to bring this marriage about ('If thou dost love fair Hero, cherish it,/ And I will break with her, and with her father,/And thou shalt have her.' 253–255), indicates that the final match is not only due to Don Pedro's authoritative status. Beatrice and Benedick's dialogue has more of a bitter and hostile touch to it, but from the romantic tradition, which still features very prominently in contemporary cinema and literature, one could come to the conclusion that they are intended for each other early on. Extremely popular films of the 20th and 21st century still employ this pattern such as *Dirty Dancing, Pretty Woman*, or *Love Actually*.

4. **You looked at the phenomenon of arranged marriages earlier on. Consider this from your point of view. Would you think it strange, if you had to marry someone you hardly knew? Imagine the conversation taking place between Antonio and Hero, when he informs her of Don Pedro's supposed intentions. How do you think she would react and how would you?**
Leonato, upon hearing from Antonio that Don Pedro intends to marry Hero, says 'I will acquaint my daughter withal, that she may be the better prepared for an answer ...' (18–20) Since this scene is not included in the play, it is obvious that Hero's previous passive and obedient behaviour continues. Leonato does not even inform Hero himself but sends Antonio, which suggests that he is not concerned about possible objections Hero might have to the marriage. In the first scene of the second act, which features Hero's next appearance on stage, the festivities already begin and Hero does not seem to have changed at all, she expresses neither concern nor joy and it seems to be a matter of fact that she will accept the Prince's offer. Thus, it is quite safe to assume that the conversation between Antonio and her is of no dramatic importance to the play, since it is probably a mere exchange of information. Antonio would report what his man overheard, might add that the information is not entirely reliable yet and that Leonato wants Hero to accept the offer. There is no indication that Hero might have anything to say about that herself.

5. **Read Don John's speeches describing himself again. He is a stereotypical villain. Do you know any other Shakespearean villains? Find out who might say similar things and compare the speeches.**
Cp. Don John's speech in 1.3.10–14/21–29 with Iago's speech in *Othello* (1.1.56–64/152–155) and Richard of Gloucester's opening soliloquy in *Richard III* (1.1.24–38).
All of these Shakespearean characters are villains *par excellence*. They do not really have an ulterior motive such as revenge, money, love etc. but dedicate themselves to evil out of pleasure. They justify this desire by referring to their particular disposition as human beings, claiming that their commitment to villainy is innate and necessarily springs from their natural character. Moreover, they all openly (i.e. to the audience) declare themselves to be villains so that nothing but evil can be expected from them. While Richard and Iago manipulate the people around them from the beginning by concealing their vicious nature, Don John must first be persuaded that he should not openly display his hatred of Don Pedro and everyone around him but that he should hide what he is, to gain the others' trust and thus be able to cause proper mischief among them.

6. **You should always keep in mind that ADO is a play, it was meant to be performed rather than read. Plays usually require 'stage directions', i.e. information for the actors what to do, where to go, when to enter the stage and when to leave it. In many plays you also find directions for facial expressions, tone of voice, etc. Collect the stage directions you can find in act 1. How much information can you gather from them?**

1.1: Enter Leonato, governor of Messina, Hero his daughter and Beatrice his niece, with a Messenger/Enter Don Pedro, Claudio, Benedick, Baithasar and John the bastard/To Don John/Exeunt all except Benedick and Claudio/Enter Don Pedro/Exit [Benedick]/Exeunt [Claudio and Don Pedro]. 1.2: Enter Leonato and an old man Antonio, brother to Leonato/Several persons cross the stage/Exeunt. I, iii: Enter Don John the bastard and Conrade his companion/Enter Borachio/Exeunt.
The stage direction 'exeunt' always marks the end of a scene, since all characters leave the stage. The other stage directions inform about the characters present on stage and indicate family relations such as daughter, niece etc. The emphasis on Antonio as 'old' is a little unusual but might be related to the dialogue between him and Ursula in 2.1. The introduction of Don John as 'the bastard' clearly singles him out and indicates that he is an outsider who might be plotting against others, since bastards in the Elizabethan Age were considered to be of a jealous and mischievous nature. 'Several persons cross the state' is supposed to emphasise what a 'busy time' it is for Leonato's household and that everyone is busy with preparations for the festivities in the evening, which is the official reason why Leonato does not talk to Hero himself about the marriage.

7. **In addition to explicit stage directions Shakespeare tends to merge indirect ones into the dialogue. Do you find any 'hidden' directions in the text? E.g. at the beginning of the play Leonato enters the stage and his first sentence is: 'I learn in this letter that Don Pedro of Aragon comes this night to Messina.' This tells you that he is holding a letter and that he might have been reading and entering the stage at the same time, although there is no stage direction telling the actor to do so. Can you find similar examples in the text?**
The Messenger's announcement 'Don Pedro is approached' in 1.1.76, prepares the audience for the addition to the stage society, indicates to the actors already present on stage to rearrange their positions, and also directs the actors behind the curtain to enter the stage now.
Beatrice's attack on Benedick (94: 'I wonder that you will still be talking') suggests that the preceding dialogue between Don Pedro and Leonato is not over but that they have stepped aside to continue it. This proves true, when Don Pedro says later on 'That is the sum of all, Leonato.' (117), which means that they obviously keep talking to each other aside during all of Benedick's and Beatrice's dialogue. Since this line is spoken out loud by Don Pedro, although he does not address the other characters on stage, it indicates that the two are walking back into the centre of the stage so that their conversation becomes audible. Don Pedro's next line ('Signor Claudio and Signor Benedick ...' 117f.) makes clear that they are now back in the centre of attention and that he addresses the rest of the company.
Don Pedro's and Leonato's movement leaves room for Beatrice and Benedick who occupy centre stage and the audience's attention during their dialogue. It becomes clear that both of them have the desire to have the last word, wherefore it is a little surprising that Benedick does not react to Beatrice's last line ('You always end with a jade's trick; I know you of old' 116). Since there is no stage direction given, this line is liable to different interpretations, such as bitterness, depending on the antecedents, or simply an interruption by Don Pedro.

Worksheet 2

What do the main characters in the first scene say about each other? Find quotations of what Beatrice says about Benedick, what Benedick says to Beatrice, Claudio about Hero and so on ...

Beatrice	**Benedick**	**Claudio**
about Benedick	about Beatrice	remarks about Hero
directed at Benedick	directed at Beatrice	
attitude towards Benedick	attitude towards Beatrice	attitude towards Hero
	remarks about Hero	
	attitude towards Hero	

Worksheet 2 Solution

Beatrice	Benedick	Claudio
about Benedick	about Beatrice	remarks about Hero
'Signor Mountanto' (25) '... four of his five wits went halting off ... now is the whole man governed with one' (52 ff.) '... every month a new sworn brother' (58) '... his faith ... the fashion of his hat' (60 f.) '... like a disease ... sooner caught than the pestilence ... caught the Benedick' (68 ff.)	'... were she not possessed with a fury, exceeds ... in beauty' (152 f.)	'... a modest young lady' (131) '... the sweetest lady that ever I looked on' (149) '... my passion change not shortly' (175) 'That I love her, I feel' (184) '... soft and delicate desires ... prompting me how fair young Hero is ... I liked her ere I went to wars' (248 f.)
directed at Benedick	directed at Beatrice	
'Courtesy itself must convert to Disdain if you come in her presence.' (98 f.) 'Scratching could not make it worse, and (= if) 'twere such a face as yours were' (109 f.)	'... some gentleman ... shall scape ... a scratched face' (107 f.) 'I would my horse had the speed of your tongue' (113)	
attitude towards Benedick	attitude towards Beatrice	attitude towards Hero
scorn (seeming) contempt	Scorn, mixed with admiration	Romantic love, not free from the usual clichés. There is dramatic irony* in the fact that he uses the word 'change' in connection with his passion, if one considers scene 4.1.
	remarks about Hero	
	'... too low for a high praise ... I do not like her' (136–140) 'Would you buy her ... ?' (143) 'Leonato's short daughter' (171)	
	attitude towards Hero	
	arrogance	

Worksheet 3

What are the specific relations between the characters listed below? Fill in the boxes with the elements that combine them and the elements that set them apart.

Leonato	Antonio

Beatrice	Hero

Benedick	Claudio

Don Pedro	Don John

Worksheet 3 Solution

What are the specific relations between the characters listed below? Fill in the boxes with the elements that combine them and the elements that set them apart.

<table>
<tr><th>Leonato</th><th>Antonio</th></tr>
<tr><td colspan="2">Elderly brothers, socially of relatively high rank, good-natured, generous</td></tr>
<tr><td>In command of his household, provides detached insight into ‘merry war’ between Beatrice and Benedick</td><td>Easily duped, describes his mistaken servant as a ‘good sharp fellow’ (1.2.15)</td></tr>
</table>

<table>
<tr><th>Beatrice</th><th>Hero</th></tr>
<tr><td colspan="2">Cousins, attractive young ladies, whose forthcoming marriage might be expected.</td></tr>
<tr><td>Very active, aggressive, emancipated, (e. g. her quarrel with Benedick)</td><td>Passive, silent throughout act 1</td></tr>
</table>

<table>
<tr><th>Benedick</th><th>Claudio</th></tr>
<tr><td colspan="2">Successful young soldiers and friends</td></tr>
<tr><td>Sceptical about women: ‘… truly I love none’ (1.1.102); ‘… a professed tyrant to their sex’ (1.1.134); continually quarreling with Beatrice</td><td>Caricature of Romantic lover;
nevertheless interested in financial aspects: ‘Hath Leonato any son my lord?’ (1.1.239)</td></tr>
</table>

<table>
<tr><th>Don Pedro</th><th>Don John</th></tr>
<tr><td colspan="2">Princes and half-brothers; the two highest-ranking persons in the play</td></tr>
<tr><td>Good-natured, benevolent, willing to bring about marriages: ‘I shall see thee … look pale with love’ (1.1.200); ‘I will assume thy part … to her father will I break.’ (1.1.266 ff.)</td><td>Social outcast, ill-natured, malicious schemer; ‘I am a plain-dealing villain’; intends to prevent marriage between Claudio and Hero at any cost (1.3.25 f.) ‘… to build mischief …’ (1.3.37)</td></tr>
</table>

Worksheet 4

Below you can see two possible stagings of scene 2.3. Think of other ways to perform this particular eavesdropping scene.

Alternative stagings for the arbour scene in Act 2, Scene 3, by C. Walter Hodges.
[a] 'Arbour' simulated simply by use of stage posts
[b] 'Arbour' as a carried-on property

Act Two

Unterrichtsempfehlungen

Die drei in vielfacher Hinsicht unterschiedlichen Szenen dieses Aktes bieten sich in besonderer Weise dazu an, Shakespeares *infinite variety* zu akzentuieren und dabei auch hinsichtlich der Unterrichtsformen zu differenzieren.
Die vorgesehenen *Activities* der langen und durch mehrfache Änderungen der Bühnengesellschaft sowie Musik, Tanz, Masken, Täuschungsmanöver und Missverständnisse höchst bewegten Szene 2.1 könnten etwa in vier Gruppen bearbeitet und von diesen anschließend mit ihren Lösungsvorschlägen zur Diskussion gestellt werden.
Themenstellungen für die einzelnen Gruppen:
1. The Structure of Scene 2.1 (See Synopsis 2.1)
2. The Theme of Appearance vs Reality (Activity 1)
3. The Continuation of the 'Merry War'
4. Claudio and Benedick Compared (Activities 2–4)

Der Strukturvergleich der Szenen 2.1 und 2.2 bietet sich für die Entwicklung eines Tafelbildes/OHP-Transparency im Rahmen eines allgemeinen Unterrichtsgepräches an (Scene 2.2, activity 1). Ähnlichkeiten der schurkischen Pläne Borachios und Iagos könnten durch eine entsprechend interessierte Spezialistengruppe erarbeitet und vorgetragen werden, möglichst unter Einsatz einer DVD/Videocassette. Diese Gruppe sollte sich mit der Tragödie *Othello* insgesamt befassen, eventuell auch über Gattungsfragen referieren und Hilfsmittel wie Internet, Literaturgeschichten und natürlich eine (eventuell zweisprachige) Textausgabe des *Othello* einsetzen.
Die Szene 2.3 bildet zweifellos einen komischen Höhepunkt, der eine detaillierte Interpretation mit dem gesamten Kurs erfordert. Wegen der besonderen Bühnenwirksamkeit empfiehlt sich auch ein Vergleich der BBC- und Branagh-Inszenierungen (Dauer: jeweils knapp 15 Min.) Im Idealfall könnte eine eigene Inszenierung durch eine Drama Group in Angriff genommen werden.

Act 2 Scene 1

Solutions

Activities p. 31

1. **The theme of appearance versus reality plays an important role in all of Shakespeare's plays and a particular one in this scene. Find and describe various examples of it, thinking of pretence, deception, error, irony, the revelation of these phenomena and the reactions of the characters on stage and the audience in the theatre.**
   1–69: Beatrice denies the idea of marriage. The audience, however, anticipates a 'happy ending', i.e. marriage with her seeming antagonist, Benedick.
   SD 70 ff.: Masks are by definition an illustration of putting on a false identity.
   94 ff.: In addition to his mask Antonio denies his identity. He is recognised nevertheless by Ursula.
   102: Her flattery 'your excellent wit' is obviously ironic, i.e. not in accordance with reality. The irony is 'signalled', i.e. made clear to the audience by the context, in which she mocks the senile Antonio.
   104 ff.: Beatrice pretends not to recognise Benedick under his mask. She scorns him, pretending to talk to someone else.
   132 ff.: Don John thinks his brother Don Pedro to be in love with Hero.

verspotten
verachten /
verschmähen

137 ff.: Claudio pretends to be Benedick, Don John pretends to believe this.
147 ff.: Claudio reveals in a soliloquy, i.e. to the audience, the discrepancy between his pretended and his true identity. He is deceived in thinking that Don Pedro has betrayed him.
162 ff.: Benedick is also convinced that Pedro has wooed for himself.
195 ff.: Benedick criticises Pedro for his seeming betrayal.
255 ff.: Pedro explains the error – 'his conceit is false' – and reveals the true situation.
311 ff.: Pedro announces his benevolent stratagem to bring Beatrice and Benedick together. The audience assumes that it will also be based on some sort of pretence, to which it is looking forward (see 2.3).
The overall effect of all this is a feeling of superiority in the audience. We are meant to recognise the various deceptions and errors and the different degrees of awareness of the characters on stage. We might identify more or less with some of them, perhaps feel pity or disgust for others. At any rate, feeling superior makes us amused, and that is one of the aims of comedy.

2. Soliloquies – Claudio's soliloquy in this scene (147–157) is one of very few moments, in which he takes centre stage – analyse his speech, which is delivered in blank verse. What does he talk about and what does this tell you about his character?
Claudio reveals his disappointment about his friend and superior, Don Pedro, whom he thinks to have deceived and betrayed him. He tends to pity himself in this situation and puts his present fate on a general level, when he utters a whole series of proverbial truisms (150 ff.), the effect being heightened by the poetry of blank verse. He concludes by bidding farewell to Hero. This resolution appears somewhat sudden after his recent enthusiasm: '... a modest young lady ... the sweetest lady that I ever looked on' (1.1.131–150). Such changes of mood are not untypical of young lovers, especially when portrayed in a Shakespearean comedy.

3. Compare Claudio's and Benedick's (174–181) reactions to the preceding dialogues, describing similarities and differences.
Benedick is no less frustrated than his friend Claudio. He has obviously been hit by by Beatrice's invections – 'the prince's jester ... dull fool ... impossible slanders ... villany' (2.1.116 ff.), insults that were seemingly uttered in front of another person, as Beatrice had pretended not to recognise Benedick behind his mask. The latter verbalises his frustration in a series of exclamations in prose: '... the prince's fool! Hah ... yea ... I'll be revenged ...' (176 ff.). He does not promise or threaten to quit her, though. So we may look forward to some more of their 'merry war'.

4. After their dance, Benedick is really offended – what exactly did Beatrice say about him to upset him?
The things that hurt Benedick the most are the ones Beatrice says about his humour. Since he fancies himself to be a funny sidekick, her implication that this leads to no one taking him seriously on the one hand offends him, but on the other hand seems to confirm his worst fears. At this point in time, he feels a little insecure, because his best friend Claudio is about to cross over to 'the other side' and Don Pedro helps him with this, wherefore Benedick feels less included than before, and the idea that it could actually be true that nobody takes him seriously thus frightens him.

5. How does Beatrice react when Don Pedro tells her that she has 'lost the heart of Signor Benedick' (237 f.)? What does this tell you about events preceding the play?
'Indeed, my lord, he lent it me a while, and I gave him use for it, a double heart for his single one: marry once before he won it of me, with false dice, therefore your grace may well say I have lost it.' (239–242) Her lines possibly imply several things: that she was in love with him, for she gave him her heart; that he wooed her, because he deliberately tried to win it off her; that in wooing her he made promises he didn't

keep or lied about things, because she speaks of 'false dice' and that he never gave her his heart, because when she gave him hers, he had 'a double one' since he kept his for himself.

6. **When the engagement between Hero and Claudio is settled, Beatrice says: 'Speak, cousin, or (if you cannot) stop his mouth with a kiss and let him not speak either.' (268 f.) Do you think Hero and Claudio kiss upon this or not? Give your reasons for whatever you assume.**
In most film productions the couple kiss at this point, because it makes the situation more romantic. In the play, however, there is not necessarily an indication that they do because the scene continues with the focus on Beatrice. And it might also be questionable whether, if they kiss, it is Hero who initiates it. It might be more realistic, if instead of Hero, Claudio takes up Beatrice's suggestion.

7. **When Don Pedro says 'Lady Beatrice, I will get you one [a husband]' (278), he basically proposes to Beatrice. Do you think he is in earnest? How does Beatrice turn him down?**
Since the whole situation is rather playful and there is no indication, either before or after this scene, that Don Pedro is seriously interested in Beatrice, it probably isn't a real proposal. Beatrice's reaction to it is very wise nonetheless, because she avoids offending him, just in case he was not joking. By flattering him and indicating that he is too good to be married to her, she turns him down without making it too obvious.

Act 2 Scene 2

Solutions

1. **Shakespeare frequently uses the technique of contrast. Illustrate this by comparing scenes 2.1. and 2.2.** Activities p. 33
2.1 is a very long scene (332 lines) with a great number of characters, many entrances and exits during the scene, masks, music dancing etc. The overall atmosphere is lively and positive. The end is marked by Don Pedro's good-natured plan to engage his friends Leonato, Claudio and Hero in a benevolent stratagem to unite the most attractive characters of the comedy, Beatrice and Benedick.
Scene 2.2 contrasts with the preceding one in many aspects. It is short (47 lines) and entirely dominated by two extremely nasty characters, accomplices of a highly negative kind, two typical Shakespearean villains, planning an ugly stratagem with the aim to ruin the reputation of an innocent bride and thereby destroying the union between another couple of principal characters, thus plunging their families into despair.

Scene 2.1	Scene 2.2
very long (332 lines)	relatively short (47 lines)
many characters, most of them positive	only two villains
lively atmosphere	sombre atmosphere
lots of movement, entrances, exits, masks, music, dancing	static
witty dialogues, mixed with soliloquies	just one dialogue, centring round single theme
positive stratagem: intention: unite a couple not yet aware of their mutual attraction	negative stratagem: intention: separate a couple who have just promised eternal love to each other

Conclusion: a good example illustrating Shakespeare's infinite variety.

2. 'Only to despite them I will endeavour anything.' (26) – What are Don John's motives for his vicious scheme?

He had claimed in act 1, scene 3 that he cannot bear the fact that Claudio is so high in Don Pedro's favour and earns honour and glory he believes to be his own. However, like most Shakespearean villains, he is not so much driven by clearly indicated motives but rather seems to fulfil his role as a bastard and thus a villain, which nature has given him. He has made various points of being melancholy and never satisfied with anything and therefore he probably cannot bear the merriness and love around him, which, for a person of his disposition, is a good enough motive of destroying the others' happiness.

3. As noted above, Shakespeare wrote another play, *Othello*, where a similar scheme makes Othello kill his wife Desdemona out of jealousy, although she is innocent. Since ADO is a comedy, you know that this won't happen but what do you think will be necessary to prevent such a tragic outcome?

At this point in the play, it might seem that Don John and his companions will be found out by a comic incident. Or, that their scheme will never actually take on and they will fail, because the merriment of everyone around them cannot be destroyed. Another course of events could be that Don John, emotionally touched by a crucial incident, changes his character and repents his former evil tendency. In this scenario, he might even also get married to someone in the end.

Act 2 Scene 3

Solutions

Activities p. 41

1. Analyse Benedick's opening soliloquy – what kind of attitude towards women does he express?

First of all, he claims that any man who falls in love, makes a fool out of himself. For this and other reasons, he claims that only the perfect woman could ever entice him and she does not exist. For the perfect woman would have to be beautiful, intelligent and virtuous. Moreover, she would have to be rich, noble, and mild. He obviously creates the perfect image of a woman here to be on the safe side – since he cannot imagine that such a woman exists, he gives himself a good enough reason to justify to himself that he will never get married. The fact that he goes to great lengths in justifying his disapproval of marriage (although he is alone), however, suggests that he does feel a certain pressure to get married. Either because everyone around him does it or because he would quite like it himself but cannot admit to it.

2. During the conversation between Leonato, Pedro and Claudio, Benedick hides but is still visible to the audience. Re-enact his reaction to what he is hearing.

Free activity.

3. What points do the three men make that convince Benedick to change his mind about Beatrice?

First of all, their statements about Beatrice's undying love for him very much flatter him. 2. they paint quite a pitiful picture of her to raise his sympathy. 3. they praise her, which makes her even more appealing in his eyes. 4. they criticise his behaviour towards her and thus make him view himself critically. 5. they flatter him and speak about his excellent judgement etc., which makes him more self-assured and he believes quite readily that Beatrice is in love with him. 6. He feels bad about his previous behaviour towards her and therefore decides to change.

4. **Compare how Leonato and Claudio talk about Benedick in contrast to the things Don Pedro says about him.**
While Claudio and Leonato make some jokes about Benedick, they also mention his positive attributes, and on the whole their conversation about Benedick is not really mean. In everything Don Pedro says, however, he tries to include some sort of offence or ridicule about Benedick. He seems determined not to let this opportunity slip by without getting back at Benedick. For what, is not quite clear.

5. **In a longer soliloquy we get to hear Benedick's reaction to the things he has just heard: summarise his thoughts.**
First of all, he does indeed believe everything that he has heard. Mostly, because the three men did a good job in keeping a serious countenance, but also because Leonato was included, and his age seems to suggest that they were actually serious. Benedick's immediate resolution is to love Beatrice back, just because she is in love with him, which seems to indicate that he has been seriously attracted to her before. He does not want to seem proud and he regrets that he has been ranting about marriage for so long. All of a sudden, the perfect woman he described just a little earlier, seems to be embodied by Beatrice and he sees absolutely no reason not to marry her. He is so determined that even the anticipated mockery by all the others for changing his opinion cannot keep him from deciding then and there to marry Beatrice.

6. **When Beatrice enters, Benedick's behaviour towards her is totally altered, which confuses her very much. If you had to instruct the actress how to behave, what would you tell her? Should she be merely confused or even angry or is she amused?**
First of all, she should be annoyed. Since in all their flirtatious banter there has been so much underlying aggression and she is wary about Benedick's criticism, his altered behaviour at this point probably feels like a trap. Thus, she is on her guard, lest she step into it and she is certainly annoyed with him for behaving this way. Since he does not change his behaviour throughout this scene though and there is no hidden agenda, some of her anger may wear off and she possibly leaves the stage simply confused.

Reviewing Act Two

Solutions

1. **This act lays the groundwork for the rest of the play. Which are the most important aspects of it?** **Activities p. 42**
The two love stories develop further, the engagement takes place and Benedick falls in love with Beatrice. The eavesdropping scene in 2.3 in particular contributes to the comedy of the play and creates the counterweight to Don John's evil scheme, which also develops further in this act. Moreover, we get more insight into the characters, i.e. Claudio's behaviour in 2.1 reveals his naïvety, Beatrice's reaction to the engagement suggests a different view of marriage than she had presented beforehand and Benedick's immediately positive reaction towards Beatrice's alleged love also seems to indicate that he is not so anti-marriage or even anti-Beatrice as he made the others believe.

2. **How do the three scenes of this act differ from one another and what are their functions?**
The merriment, movement and comedy of scenes 1 and 3 form a frame around the static and grave atmosphere of scene 2. The dynamics of scene 1 with all the dancing

and many changes in the stage society sets the proper comic mood after many introductory elements in act 1. Scene 2 develops the dark aspect of the play further but due to the following eavesdropping scene the general comic tone is maintained.

3. **In particular scenes 1 and 3 are characterised by means such as masking and eavesdropping. How do these elements influence the plotlines?**
In scene 1, the masks serve several important purposes. 1) The general theme of appearance vs. reality is emphasised. 2) Don John's interference is made possible through the masks. 3) A crucial moment in the relationship between Beatrice and Benedick also depends on the fact that he is masked and does not know that she knows who he is. In scene 3, the comedy of the eavesdropping scene restores the light tone of the play after a rather dark scene. Moreover, the method Leonato, Pedro and Claudio employ makes their story more credible for Benedick than if they had merely told him and thus, he falls in love immediately.

4. **Given all the confusion and mistaking which has happened so far, do you think Don John's scheme is going to work out the way he wants?**
Scene 1 clearly demonstrates that Claudio will be easy prey for Don John, because he is too naïve to question things and thus one can assume that Don John's scheme will work very well. Moreover, the society of Messina provides Don John with perfect conditions for creating confusion and dissent due to such things as masques and eavesdropping scenes etc.

5. **Compare Benedick's opening soliloquy in scene 3 with his soliloquy towards the end of the scene – what are the main differences?**
The two speeches are very parallel but include vital differences. In the opening soliloquy Benedick mocks Claudio for having turned from soldier to lover, i. e. from man to fool and he describes his ideal of a woman, implying that he would not marry anyone who falls short of this ideal. In the soliloquy at the end of the scene, he has turned from soldier to lover himself and he is aware of it, for he anticipates the mockery he himself applied earlier. He knows that he acts incoherently but his desire for Beatrice is stronger than the fear of being exposed to ridicule. Moreover, his view of Beatrice very much sounds like his earlier description of the ideal woman: 'they say the lady is fair, 'tis a truth, I can bear them witness: and virtuous, 'tis so, I cannot reprove it: and wise, but for loving me ...' (2.3.202–204)

6. **Summarise briefly each of the three scenes. These summaries will give you an idea of the three main plotlines of ADO. What are those?**
In scene 2.1 the love plot centering around Claudio and Hero is developed. Don Pedro woos Hero in Claudio's name, but due to the interference of Don John, Claudio is misled into thinking that Don Pedro is in love with Hero himself. Only when all characters of the stage society get together towards the end of the scene is the misunderstanding cleared up and Claudio and Hero get engaged. Scene 2 consists of the further development of the scheme laid out by Don John and Borachio to prevent the marriage. Borachio acquaints Don John with his plan of leading Claudio to believe that Hero has had premarital sex in order to break up the engagement. Scene 3 is part of the love plot focusing on Beatrice and Benedick. Whilst he is eavesdropping on Don Pedro, Claudio and Don Leonato, Benedick is led to believe that Beatrice is in love with him, which confuses but also excites him and he falls in love with her too.
The three scenes of act 2 thus represent the three different plots (two love plots and an evil scheme) which will develop throughout the rest of the play.

x 7. **Two different schemes are planned in this act by two different parties – compare the schemes and the parties' motives.**

While one is good-natured with a lot of comic potential, the other is ill-natured and has rather tragic than comic potential. The scheme laid out by Don Pedro etc. is created to further the romantic plot, whereas the scheme laid out by Don John has the exact opposite as its basis.

8. **What have you learnt about the different characters from this act that you didn't know before? Gather together statements made by Beatrice, Benedick, Hero and Claudio, which seem to you to be typical of the respective character.**

Benedick	Beatrice
'The prince's fool! Hah, it may be I go under that title because I am merry: yea but so I am apt to do myself wrong: I am not so reputed, it is the base (though bitter) disposition of Beatrice, that puts the world into her person and so gives me out: well, I'll be revenged as I may.' (2.1.177–181) 'I would not marry her, though she were endowed with all that Adam had left him before he transgressed.' (2.1.215–217) '... till all graces be in one woman, one woman shall not come in my grace' (2.3.25/26) 'I will be horribly in love with her' (2.3.205/206) 'The world must be peopled ...' (2.3.211/212) 'When I said I would die a bachelor, I did not think I should live till I were married.' (2.3.212/213)	'He that hath a beard is more than a youth: and he that hath no beard is less than a man: and he that is more than a youth, is not for me, and he that is less than a man, I am not for him.' (2.1.29–32) '... it is my cousin's duty to make curtsy, and say, father, as it please you: but yet for all that, cousin, let him be a handsome fellow, or else make another curtsy, and say, father, as it please me.' (2.1.43–46) 'Indeed, my Lord, he lent it me a while, and I gave him use for it, a double heart for his single one: marry once before he won it of me, with false dice.' (2.1.239–242) 'Thus goes every one to the world but I, and I am sunburnt, I may sit in a corner and cry, 'Heigh ho for a husband'.' (2.1.275–277)
Claudio	**Hero**
'Friendship is constant in all other things, Save in the office and affairs of love ...' (2.1.150/151) '... beauty is a witch, Against whose charms faith melteth into blood' (2.1.154/155) 'Silence is the perfectest herald of joy, I were but little happy if I could say how much!' (2.1.264/265)	'I will do any modest office, my lord, to help my cousin to a good husband.' (2.1.322/323)

9. **In which way does music play a significant part in this act? How does it function? Also, think of Benedick's comparison of soldiers and lovers and their musical preferences at the beginning of scene 3 (12–14).**

First of all, the music here contributes to the light-hearted tone suitable for comedy in general but also suitable for this scene in particular, for the funny and romantic streak of the play is most prevalent in this scene. Secondly, the song that is being played, draws on the overall theme of ADO: 'Men were deceivers ever.' (2.3.57) Benedick, in particular, makes frequent references throughout the play to certain musical clichés, such as that people in love like different music than soldiers: 'I have known when there was no music with him but the drum and fife, and now had he rather hear the tabor and the pipe.' (2.3.12–14) The fact that Balthasar plays a piece of that music that Benedick ascribes only to lovers and fools, not 'real' men, already suggests that Benedick himself will be turned into one of those.

Worksheet 5

Shakespeare's Language

Although early modern English, Shakespeare's English, is very close to contemporary English, it still includes some forms that are now extinct. Early modern English, for example, has two pronouns for the second person singular, whereas contemporary English only has 'you.' Similarly, verbs still had inflected endings in the second person singular. The syntax was also different, for example in negations or in questions. Look at the dialogue between Hero and Ursula in scene 3.1. Find all the forms that are today extinct and write them in the matching box below. Then rephrase the sentences according to the standard in contemporary English.

	Early Modern English	**Contemporary English**
2nd person singular pronoun		
Inflected endings		
Syntax		
Other (missing prepositions etc.)		

Worksheet 5 Solution

Shakespeare's Language

Although early modern English, Shakespeare's English is very close to contemporary English, it still includes some forms that are now extinct. Early modern English, for example, has two pronouns for the second person singular, whereas contemporary English only has 'you.' Similarly, verbs still had inflected endings in the second person singular. The syntax was also different, for example in negations or in questions. Look at the dialogue between Hero and Ursula in scene 3.1. Find all the forms that are today extinct and write them in the matching box below. Then rephrase the sentences according to the standard in contemporary English.

	Early Modern English	Contemporary English
2nd person singular pronoun	run thee (1) thou (2) thou (6) thy office (12) bear thee well in it (13) thy part (18) my talk to thee (20) I'll show thee (102) thy counsel (102) I will requite thee (111) To thy loving hand (112) If thou (113)	run you you your task do a good job your part what I say to you I'll show you your counsel I will love you back to your loving hand If you
Inflected endings	There shalt thou (2) thou overheard'st (6) when Beatrice doth come (15) If thou dost love (113) Thou dost deserve (115)	There will you you overheard when Beatrice comes If you love me You deserve
Syntax	run thee ... (1) There shalt thou find (2) So angle we for Beatrice (29) Fear you not (31) Then go we near her (32) So says the prince (38) So turns she every man (68) be not angry with me (94) Stand I condemned (108)	run There you will find So do we angle for Beatrice Do not be afraid Then we should go near her The prince says so So does she turn every man don't be angry with me Do I stand condemned
Other (missing prepositions etc.)	Whisper her ear (4) To listen our purpose (12) doth (15) Why did you so (44)	Whisper into her ear To listen to our plan does Why did you do so

Act Three

Unterrichtsempfehlungen

Der 3. Akt ist mit fünf Szenen, der Konversion Beatrices, der Verspottung des gewandelten Benedick und Weiterführung der Intrige Don Johns, der Einführung der farcenhaft überzeichneten Ordnungshüter, der Verhaftung der Übeltäter, den Hochzeitsvorbereitungen und schließlich der Fast-Aufklärung der bösartigen Verschwörung der bewegteste Akt der Komödie, zugleich deren strukturelles Zentrum.
Da die Szene 3.1 quasi ein inhaltliches Pendant der zuvor intensiv behandelten Szene 2.3 darstellt, kann hier die Diskussionsleitung weitgehend auf eine entsprechend präparierte Schülergruppe übergehen. Ziel sollte sein, die zahlreichen strukturellen Ähnlichkeiten, aber auch Unterschiede zwischen beiden Szenen tabellarisch zusammenzufassen. Auch hier erscheint ein Vergleich der DVD-Produktionen von BBC und Branagh ratsam.
Zusätzlich oder alternativ kann hier unter Einsatz von Worksheet No. 5 ein Exkurs zu Shakespeares Sprache eingeschoben werden.
Die Szene 3.2 kann kursorisch behandelt werden. Von besonderem Interesse ist der abrupte atmosphärische Bruch, bewirkt durch das Erscheinen Don Johns und den damit verbundenen Themenwechsel von der Verspottung Benedicks zu Johns finsteren Machenschaften.
Vor Behandlung der Straßenszene 3.3 empfehlen sich Schülerreferate zu den Begriffen *farce, caricature, malapropism*. Die Interpretationsleitung könnten anschließend dieselben Schüler übernehmen. Auch diese Szene lädt ein zu einer Amateurproduktion durch eine Drama Group, wobei vorzugsweise rustikalere Schülertypen zum Einsatz kämen.
Die unmittelbaren Hochzeitsvorbereitungen (3.4) mit Gesprächen über Mode und sexuellen Anspielungen lassen sich durchaus kursorisch behandeln. Ähnliches gilt für den clownesken Aufklärungsversuch Leonatos durch die Ordnungshüter (3.5), welcher an deren sprachlichem und sonstigem Unvermögen und der Eile des aufgeregten Brautvaters scheitert.

Act 3 Scene 1

Solutions

Activities p. 46

1. Analyse the conversation between Hero and Ursula. They employ several means to make Beatrice consider Benedick – which can you identify?
First of all, they pretend that Benedick is in love with her already, which makes it easier for her to admit to her own feelings. Secondly, by calling Beatrice 'too disdainful' (34) and 'wild' (35), they try to weaken her self-confidence and make her question her behavior. They also refer to the fact that she thinks too highly of herself ('her wit/Values itself so highly that to her/All matter else seems weak.' 52–54) in order to humble her a little, which is necessary for her to open up emotionally. Apart from that, Hero says of Beatrice that 'she cannot love' (54), which most likely has the immediate effect that Beatrice would like to prove Hero wrong. Thirdly, they talk about Benedick's alleged suffering in order to cause Beatrice's sympathy ('Therefore let Benedick like covered fire,/Consume away in sighs, waste inwardly.' 77/78). Fourthly, they flatter her and appeal to her vanity: 'She cannot be so much without true judge-

ment,/Having so swift and elegant a wit/As she is prized to have, as to refuse/So rare a gentleman as Signor Benedick' (88–91). They are thus indicating that if Beatrice is as clever as she fancies herself to be, she must fall in love with Benedick, which she immediately does. Fifthly, they praise Benedick as a good-looking, intelligent, witty man.

2. **How do you imagine the dynamics of this scene? How do Hero and Ursula change the volume of their voices according to what they are saying? How do you imagine Beatrice's reactions whilst eavesdropping? At the end, Ursula is convinced that their stratagem was successful – how can she be so sure? Imagine what Beatrice might look like.**
One could stage the scene with Hero and Ursula pacing up and down in front of a row of bushes or a hedge, which Beatrice hides behind, so that both parties are visible to the audience. Whenever they include little side blows concerning Beatrice's character they could emphasise them more by raising their voices in her direction as to make sure that she'll understand, which adds a comic effect. During the first half of the conversation, Beatrice could be really eager to hear everything and very active, making sure that she catches every word. To demonstrate that this stratagem does have a profound effect on her, she could slow down progressively during the conversation, until she seems deep in thought, like in a trance, not noticing anything. That could support Ursula's statement at the end of the dialogue, when she takes a closer look at Beatrice, who does not even notice.

3. **Analyse Beatrice's final speech in this scene. Which is the form and what exactly does she say?**
The scene is concluded with a shortened sonnet (two quatrains instead of three, rhyming abab, cdcd – plus a rhyming couplet), which is used to demonstrate that now the love plot centred around the two couples fades a little into the background for dramatic purposes. From the next scene on, the darker side of the story becomes prevalent. The first stanza shows the effect Hero's and Margaret's criticism had on Beatrice. She feels it strongly and is ashamed of herself, vowing to change her behaviour. The second stanza hints at the future development, for she claims that she'll be in love with Benedick too and will marry him. In the couplet she draws on two important general aspects of the play: appearance vs reality. She says that she believes the reports about what Benedick is like, but more importantly she claims that she intuitively knows this already, so that she doesn't have to rely on the reports, which is always a dangerous thing to do, as it turns out in the next scene

Act 3 Scene 2

Solutions

Activities p. 50

1. **From one day to the other, Benedick is a changed man. Read the dialogue between Don Pedro and Claudio again, who mock Benedick for the change. What is different about him and what does that tell you about how he looked before?**
He is said to be 'sadder' (13), i.e. more serious or even melancholic, which is the common habit of an unrequited or not yet requited lover. He wears very different clothes, which are long and loose. This emphasises his transformation from soldier to lover, since clothes as these make it impossible to ride a horse, let alone fight. His general appearance is a lot cleaner ("a brushes his hat o'mornings' (35); 'And when was he wont to wash his face?' (47)), which means that he puts effort in that he didn't deem necessary as a soldier. His use of perfume and cosmetics make his

transformation seem even more ridiculous. He also shaved his beard, which is typical of a lover, but also alludes to Beatrice's comment in 2.1.25 ('Lord, I could not endure a husband with a beard on his face!').

2. **Consider Claudio's reaction to Don John's statement about Hero – why does he never question the truth of it?**
As quickly as Claudio fell in love in the first act, as quickly does he fall out of it now. The repeated references in the play to his age gain more relevance now, because it is obvious that due to his youth, Claudio is too liable to rely on other people. The fact that he does not even like or generally trust Don John but believes this rather outstanding story, lessens his likeability considerably. Furthermore, he is determined to shame Hero in front of everyone else on their wedding day ('If I see anything tonight why I should not marry her tomorrow in the congregation, where I should wed, there will I shame her.' 101–103). It seems rather cruel to expose her like that, even if it were true that she is unfaithful. However, the general rashness that Claudio displays here may be ascribed to his youth. Don Pedro's equal reaction, however, is really surprising, since he is older and should know better than to trust his villainous brother.

3. **The dialogue between Don John and Don Pedro and Claudio is difficult to act out, since he must appear trustworthy to them, although we know that he is a villain – try it yourselves and act out this part of the scene.**
Free activity

Act 3 Scene 3

Solutions

Activities p. 55

1. **The rest of the stage society is introduced: the Watch. The character of constable Dogberry is still famous today for his malapropisms, which are sometimes also called 'Dogberryisms'. Identify as many of Dogberry's malapropisms as you can. What do the words have in common?**

salvation	damnation
desertless	deserving
senseless	sensible
comprehend	apprehend
vagrom	vagrant
tolerable	intolerable
vigitant	vigilant

In the attempt to advance his status and to seem well-educated, Dogberry tries to use as many difficult words as possible but clearly fails, which makes him seem even dumber. By choosing words that sound somewhat like the ones he needs, most of the time he ends up saying exactly the opposite, thus creating puns unconsciously, in contrast to the higher classes of the stage society, who do this deliberately.

Activities p. 56

2. **Dogberry, as constable the head of the watch, gives orders how his watchmen should behave when on duty. What sort of orders does he give and what is the effect of that?**
'How if a will not stand? – Why then, take no note of him, but let him go, and presently call the rest of the watch together, and thank God you are rid of a knave.' (25–27); 'True, and they are to meddle with none but the prince's subjects.' (30/31);

'We will rather sleep than talk; we know what belongs to a watch. – For I cannot see how sleeping should offend.' (34/35, 37); 'Well, you are to call at all the ale houses, and bid those that are drunk get them to bed. – How if they will not? – Why then, let them alone till they are sober.' (38–42); 'If you meet a thief, you may suspect him, by virtue of your office, to be no true man. And for such kind of men, the less you meddle or make with them, why, the more is for your honesty.' (46–49); 'The most peaceable way for you, if you do take a thief, is to let him show himself what he is, and steal out of your company.' (53–55); 'the watch ought to offend no man, and it is an offence to stay a man against his will.' (72/73)
Due to his chaotic thinking, the watch end up with no duties whatsoever. The guidelines he tries to lay out for them, render all his orders absurd. He does think logically but since he takes all things literally, he winds up without any results. Under the circumstances, it is surprising that his watchmen actually manage to arrest Conrade and Borachio.

3. **If you consider the inabilities of the watchmen and Borachio's drunkenness, how would you imagine the scene of the arrest to take place? Try to act it out.**
Quite possibly, the watchmen are determined and hesitant at the same time, attempting a little cowardly to get a hold of the two men, who, in their drunkenness probably try to defend themselves or flee. There is certainly a lot of tumult on stage during the scene.

Act 3 Scene 4

Solutions

Activities p. 59

1. **In this scene, Margaret's role is considerably more noticeable – why?**
She has more speaking lines than Hero or Beatrice and she has developed a wit which also equals Beatrice's. She takes the liberty of making sexual allusions about the impending marriage of her mistress Hero (''Twill be heavier soon by the weight of a man.' 24) and also in reference to Beatrice ('A maid and stuffed! There's goodly catching of cold.' 56). She alludes to the developing love story between Beatrice and Benedick ('Get you some of this distilled carduus benedictus, and lay it to your heart' 63/64) and her plays-on-words equal Beatrice's former ones (as in ll. 26 ff.; 68 ff.). Beatrice notices this herself: 'O, God help me, God help me, how long have you professed this apprehension?' Margaret's reply 'Ever since you left it.' (57–59) has an important dramatic implication. Since Beatrice is now in love and somewhat humbled, she is not as self-confident as before, which has to be reflected in her speech too. In terms of credibility, she needs to slow it down for a couple of scenes but the speed and wit of the previous scenes must be maintained for entertainment purposes. Thus, Shakespeare basically transfers Beatrice's comic function to Margaret for a couple of scenes. The parallel between the two is also indicated by the last two sentences of their dialogue ('What pace is that thy tongue keeps? – Not a false gallop.' 79/80) which reminds us of Benedick's statement in 1.1.113: 'I would my horse had the speed of your tongue ...'

2. **Shakespeare's plays have been adapted to the screen many times. Sometimes they have been modernized and there are several American Romantic comedies set at high schools etc., which are based on a Shakespearean comedy. For instance, 'Ten Things I Hate About You' is such a comedy, starring the late Heath Ledger, which is based on Shakespeare's *The Taming of the Shrew*. Imagine ADO as such a comedy. Think, for example, of scene 4 in act 3. It is the morning before the wedding and Hero, Ursula, Margaret and Beatrice prepare themselves. Imagine this was a mod-**

ern Romantic comedy: rewrite the dialogue as you imagine a screenwriter would adapt this scene.

Hero: Ursula, please, go wake up Beatrice, and tell her to come.

Ursula: Sure, I'll be back.

Margaret: Are you absolutely sure about your wedding dress? I thought the other one was nicer.

Hero: I am absolutely sure. I knew that this was my dress when I first saw it.

Margaret: But I think Beatrice also preferred the other one ...

Hero: Clearly, you are both stupid. This dress is perfect and I wouldn't want to wear any other for the world.

Margaret: Well it is a really nice dress. And it is totally fashionable. I saw one just like it in 'Vogue' last week.

Hero: Wow, that must have been even more gorgeous.

Margaret: Oh no, it was nothing compared to yours! It did have a beautiful long skirt and embroidery all over the top and the most beautiful veil but yours is ten times as pretty.

Hero: I hope it'll make me feel better once I'm wearing it, I'm so nervous!

Margaret: Well, just look forward to tonight. He'll give you something else to think about ...

Hero: Margaret! You have such a dirty mind!

Margaret: That's not dirty, it's the truth. After all, this is going to be your wedding night ... Ask Beatrice, I'm sure she will back me up on this.

Hero: Good morning, Beatrice.

Beatrice: Good morning, Hero.

Hero: What's wrong? You look ill!

Beatrice: Thanks a lot. But I certainly feel ill.

Margaret: Don't you mean you feel sick? Lovesick maybe?

Beatrice: Hero, isn't it time you were ready? You don't want to be late for your own wedding now, do you? God, I really don't feel well.

Margaret: What do you need? Tea, a bath, or maybe a husband?

Beatrice: What are you talking about?

Margaret: Oh, nothing of consequence. But I think you might feel better really soon ...

Hero: Look, how beautifully the gloves match the dress! I'm so glad I got them.

Beatrice: Oh my God, Hero, I think I'm gonna be sick.

Margaret: Sickness in the morning? You know what they say ... I wonder whether you might have caught more than just a cold.

Beatrice: What are you insinuating? And why do you keep teasing me incessantly? I usually do that to other people!

Margaret: Well someone has to do it and you have been neglecting this particular duty lately ... And I'm pretty good at it too, don't you think?

Beatrice: It's probably best you practise a bit more – I feel too sick to do it anyway.

Margaret: Maybe you should take some medicine. I've heard that in your case BeneVicks will help. Have you heard of it? It's especially good for your heart ...

Hero: Margaret, stop teasing her about that.

Beatrice: BeneVicks? I have never heard of that! What are you talking about? Why BENEVicks? What are you insinuating?

Margaret: I'm not insinuating anything. I'm only talking about medicine but you seem to think I'm talking about Benedick. I never thought you were in love with him but you seem to think you're in love with him. The way you react to everything I say which might only remotely be related to Benedick. And why shouldn't you be in love with him? Since clearly, he is in love with you. Just think about how much you altered him! He was always such a confirmed bachelor and he swore he would never marry but look what you've done to him! Now marriage is all he can think about!

Beatrice: You can't possibly be serious!
Margaret: Oh but I am. Just you see for yourself once we get to church!
Ursula: Hero, Beatrice, we really need to get a move on! Everyone's waiting already and though it is fashionable for the bride to be late, you surely don't want to miss your own wedding, do you?
Hero: Oh my God, I completely forgot the time. Beatrice, Margaret, help me dress, quick, quick!

Act 3 Scene 5

Solution

In this scene, the plot laid out by Don John is almost revealed. Why do you think Shakespeare included the scene? Activity p. 61

Apart from the fact that it offers additional comic value due to Dogberry's appearance, it creates dramatic suspense. If Dogberry were not so fond of complicated expressions and did not tire his interlocutor as much, he could have explained to Don Leonato whom they have arrested and why, thus preventing the following almost tragic scene. Since the audience knows about the plot, they wait for its revelation and solution. By including the scene the suspense about the happy ending is increased.

Reviewing Act Three

Solutions

1. **Summarise essential elements of act 3 comparing the five scenes with regard to setting, stage-society, length, language, themes, atmosphere, genre.** Activities p. 61

3.1 Orchard (5), the three major female characters of the play: Hero, Beatrice, Margaret, 116 lines, all in verse, elaborate imagery (8 ff., 26 ff., 107 ff.), good-natured stratagem of preceding scene echoed, Beatrice's conversion. Pleasant atmosphere, funny, high comedy.
3.2 Leonato's house, 112 lines, all in prose, 5 characters, all male, one of them being the villain of the piece, who enters later (67) and dramatically changes themes and atmosphere. Before: humourous teasing of Benedick and his changed appearance and behaviour. After the villain's entry: nasty slander, which might lead to melodramatic catastrophe.
3.3 Open air, 1–84: Dogberry and his men, all rather clownish, none of them has appeared so far; farcical language, full of malapropisms. Then Don John's villainous companions talk about the acting out of their ugly scheme, which must have happened between 3.2 and 3.3. Their melodramatic arrest. Mixture of low, farcical comedy and dramatic thriller.
3.4 Hero's apartment, Hero and her waiting women, later (28) joined by Beatrice. 84 lines, all in prose; wedding-preparations. The teasing of Beatrice corresponds to Benedick's treatment by his friends in 3.2. Light-hearted comedy.
3.5 The governor's residence. Clownish characters clash with high-ranking father of the bride; 56 lines, all in prose. Long-winded story, full of malapropisms again, contrasts with Leonato's impatient longing to attend his daughter's wedding. The clowns report on their successful arrest of the villains. Mixture of low comedy and thrilling action. Hint at happy ending, characteristic of comedy.
Conclusion: Act 3, forming the centre of the play, has the highest number of scenes.

The clownish characters complete the stage-society, with the exception of the friar, who appears in the next scene. The act abounds in dramatic contrasts and comic parallels. High comedy clashes with farce and melodramatic villainy. Good-natured tricks and humourous teasing of Benedick is echoed in the treatment of Beatrice.

2. **Throughout act 3, the two plotlines of Beatrice and Benedick's love of each other and the developing tragedy around Hero and Claudio are very closely intertwined. Write a summary of act 3 to see how quickly the two themes alternate.**
The act begins with the love scheme laid out for Beatrice. She is eavesdropping on Hero and Ursula in this scene, and she, upon hearing that Benedick supposedly loves her, falls in love with him too. Scene 2 can be divided into two parts: in the first one, Claudio and Pedro mock Benedick for his lovesick behaviour. Benedick here already speaks to Don Leonato because he would like to marry Beatrice and at the same time, Don John approaches Claudio, slandering Hero. By the end of scene 2, the love story between Beatrice and Benedick is progressing fast and, at the same time, the love between Claudio and Hero seems doomed, because he has already decided to disgrace her. In scenes 3 and 5, the interference of the watch seems likely to bring about a resolution, but when Don Leonato won't hear them out at the end of the act, Hero's wedding preparations in the scene before seem even more cynical. In this scene, while Hero is about to be married, she and Ursula also seize the opportunity of mocking Beatrice, who seems very unhappy about her newly discovered love for Benedick.

3. **At the beginning of act 3, Hero is much more active than before, so that one can get an idea of what her character might be like. How would you characterise her according to scene 1?**
The scene clearly demonstrates Hero's tendency to subordinate herself to her father, because she is never as lively as here, when he is not around. She takes delight in deceiving Beatrice, which might also have to do with the fact that usually Beatrice is superior to her. Her independence and outspokenness are very much in contrast to Hero's pleasing behaviour and this might make Hero feel inferior at times, wherefore this scene might be taken as the perfect opportunity to get back at Beatrice without actually hurting her. Not only does she feel superior here because she deceives Beatrice, but she also takes her chance to criticise Beatrice. However, she does not do so cruelly, for the things she says about her are harsh, but still true and a necessary humbling for Beatrice. Although Hero seems more active and independent in this scene than before, one has to keep in mind that she still acts on her father's will and not her own. She carries out the plot planned by the men and not her own. Moreover, she affirms their idea of marrying Beatrice off to Benedick, thus limiting her independence.

4. **One central aspect of this act is that Don John follows his plan of ruining the marriage – why is it so easy for him to deceive Don Pedro and Claudio, although they did not seem to trust him before?**
On the one hand, the fact that Don Pedro brought Don John with him to Messina and the fact that there has been no scene so far where the previous conflict would have been discussed, indicates that Don Pedro has a very forgiving nature. Despite the fact that only martial measures seemed sufficient to resolve their conflict, he gives no indication of any mistrust or suspicion of Don John anywhere in the preceding scenes. Claudio, on the other hand, is very much under the influence of Don Pedro and at the same time displays a tendency to believe things too easily. When Don John tried to make him believe that Don Pedro actually wooed Hero for himself at the ball, he had no proof of this whatsoever but chose to believe Don John anyway. Maybe his youth is supposed to account for these sudden changes of mind, which resemble also the way he fell in love with Hero in the first place.

5. If you remember that 'fashion' means clothes on the one hand but also pretending something, you will find that in this act both meanings are strongly featured – especially in scenes 2 and 4. In which way is fashion referred to in these scenes and what is the function of the theme here?

Activities p. 62

In scene 2, the numerous references to fashion draw attention to a changed Benedick. This is important for two reasons: first of all, this alludes to the ever present conflict between appearance and reality and the fact that appearances, especially of people, can be deceptive. Benedick is in love but that does not make him a different man. However, the second aspect refers to the several gender roles depicted in the play. Earlier on, Benedick had made the distinction between soldier and lover, claiming first of all that a man can never be both at the same time and secondly, that the lover is a fool. By turning into a lover himself and behaving the way he does, at first sight it seems that he affirms this statement. However, by challenging Claudio out of love for Beatrice later on, he contradicts these stereotyped perceptions.
In scene 4, Hero's dress is judged according to all elements of contemporary fashion. The direct discussion of fashion immediately before the wedding introduces the general misapprehension that will follow.

6. In this act, Dogberry and his watch are introduced – why do you think this happens in act 3, rather than 1 or 2 and what do you consider their overall function to be?

In act 1 and act 2, the groundwork for the play as a whole is laid. The characters are introduced, two possible couples are established and the conflict is announced. From these basics the story can fully develop now. Dogberry and his watch do not have a central function in the play; they are more of comic sidekicks, which is why they are introduced later, after the important elements have already been established. Their function can be compared to the element of comic relief in Shakespearean tragedy. With the development of events, which sometimes draw on tragic elements, the characters around Dogberry are used to remind us time and again that this is a comedy and will remain a comedy. Their crucial role in the resolution of the conflict is also typical of comedy, since this underlines that the conflict itself is not as severe as in a tragedy, for instance.

7. In this act, both Benedick and Claudio are in love – in what respect does their behaviour differ? Which of the two has stronger feelings for his lady? Give reasons for your opinion.

Once the engagement between Claudio and Hero has been established, Claudio does not seem to be thinking about her all that much. His behaviour has not changed and he fully concentrates on the scheme laid out for Benedick. After the engagement, he does not mention Hero and he seems neither nervous nor excited about the impending wedding. Benedick on the other hand really feels the change of his heart. He describes himself as being 'turned over' and in some sense he is. His outward appearance and his behaviour have changed. He cares more about his looks and is in a more serious mood. The news of Beatrice's love for him has deeply affected him, not least because he truly loves her back. He is a much more honest and sincere lover than Claudio, who falls in and out of love quite easily.

8. The act begins with Benedick's changed behaviour and ends with Beatrice's. Why are both so shaken and confused, even depressed?

With both characters, a lot of the comedy they create around themselves is a means of keeping other people at a distance out of fear of getting hurt. Despite their seeming self-confidence, they feel the need to distance themselves from others and the news that someone is actually in love with them deeply impresses them both. At the same time it scares them, for they know that now they will have to open up to someone else and risk getting hurt. Being in love almost terrifies them both.

Act Four

Unterrichtsempfehlungen

Der Behandlung von 4.1 könnten wiederum kurze Schülerreferate vorangestellt werden, diesmal zu den Stichworten *melodrama, coup de théâtre, deus ex machina*. Ferner könnte eine Gruppe es übernehmen, strukturelle Parallelen zwischen ADO und *Romeo and Juliet* herauszuarbeiten, insbesondere hinsichtlich der diversen Friars, die in beiden Stücken als listenreiche Freunde und Helfer auftreten, in ADO als sehr spät eingeführter Problemlöser, quasi ein *deus ex machina*, wohingegen der Retter in *Romeo and Juliet* sich tragisch verspätet, weshalb Sir Peter Ustinov diese Tragödie bezeichnet als „a comedy that has gone wrong".
Der bei heutigen Schülern verbreiteten Skepsis gegenüber dem in ADO hoch gehandelten Wert pränuptialer Virginität lässt sich wohl durch Hinweise auf andere Zeiten und Kulturen begegnen, in denen auch heute noch „Ehrenmorde" ihre Rolle spielen.
Die Gerichtsszene 4.2 lädt zur Reaktivierung der 3.3-Spezialisten (*malapropism, farce, caricature, parody*) ein. Ferner könnte sich jemand mit dem Begriff *comic relief* befassen, etwa im Hinblick auf den Porter in *Macbeth*, Clowns in *King Lear* und *Othello*, Gravediggers in *Hamlet*. Neben reichlichem Gebrauch von *malapropisms* und Dogberrys insistierendem Verlangen, als „ass" aktenkundig zu werden, verblüfft auch die Vorverurteilung des Delinquenten: „I do not like thy look" (3.2.38).
Nachdem in 4.1 mit Friar Francis die Bühnengesellschaft vervollständigt ist, bietet sich ein Exkurs über die Länge der einzelnen Rollen sowie die Verteilung der Auftritte der Figuren in der Komödie an (s. Worksheet No. 6). Das Lösungsblatt kann als Grundlage der Rollenverteilung für eine Amateurproduktion von ADO dienen.

Act 4 Scene 1

Solutions

Activities p. 73

1. **The first scene of act 4 signifies a crucial turning-point in the play. From this scene on, the play could continue as tragedy, comedy or melodrama. What do you think will happen next? Construe two possible endings to the plot from here, a comic and a tragic one.**
   For the comic plot it is obviously necessary that Don John's scheme is revealed. Claudio and Don Pedro must find out that they have been deceived but they must also repent how easily they were led astray. Hero's honour must be restored and Don John arrested as the villain that he is. Beatrice and Benedick will find a way to get together, most likely due to his help in redeeming Hero. The love story between Hero and Claudio, however, does not necessarily have a happy ending, even if the play continues as a comedy. Claudio has used her so badly that it is not foreseeable whether she will forgive him the way she eventually does.
   Assuming a tragic or melodramatic ending, several deaths might follow this scene. Hero could either die or be confined to a nunnery. Several duels are possible, e.g. Claudio and Don Leonato, Claudio and Benedick, Don Pedro and Don Leonato. Benedick might die in the attempt to redeem Hero and Beatrice would suffer violently from his death. Don Pedro would not be found and arrested but would probably get away unscathed. For a true tragedy, Claudio would find out after Hero's death that he wronged her and therefore commit suicide out of repentance.

2. **In act 3, scene 2, Claudio swore to shame Hero in the congregation, should she 'prove' disloyal and he makes good on his promise in this scene – what do you think of this behaviour?**
   Claudio claims that Hero is 'but the sign and semblance of her honour.' (31) He indicates that there is a discrepancy between the pretended and the true character of a person. This has also to do with the social rank of a person: 'O, what authority and show of truth/Can cunning sin cover itself withal.' (33/34) Since Don Leonato is such a well-respected person, everyone tends to believe that he is honourable inside and that therefore his daughter is virtuous, but this does not necessarily have to be true.
   Interestingly enough, although Claudio complains about 'exterior shows' (38) and the unreliability of outward appearance, he relies on one himself: he takes the fact that Hero blushes as evidence for her guilt. Hero's question 'And seemed I ever otherwise to you?' (52) triggers his outrage: 'Out on thee seeming!' (53) He believes that there is a strong discrepancy between what Hero seems ('You seem to me ...' 54) and what she is ('you are ...' 56). His emphasis on the opposition between appearance and reality is even more ironic, since all the evidence he has is based on what he believed to see when Borachio and Margaret performed their deceptive show.

3. **What does Leonato first think when Claudio claims that Hero has lost her virginity?**
   He believes that some time between their engagement and the wedding Hero and Claudio spent the night together, because they could not wait. Why he would think that Claudio could announce that on their wedding day in front of the whole congregation is a bit of a mystery.

4. **One of the major themes of this play, the opposition between appearance and reality, features very prominently in this scene. Find out which aspects are mentioned and by whom.**
   Not only does Claudio cause a scene on account of things he believes to know but he also constantly draws attention to his belief that nothing is as it seems, although he is the one, who is so deceived. He claims that Hero is a 'rotten orange' (30), i. e. bad on the inside, not on the outside, and that she is 'but the sign and semblance of her honour.' (31) For the audience, who know the truth, this merely emphasises the deception he has fallen for. When Hero blushes, he takes this is as a confirmation of her infidelity. The errors in judgement that are made due to outward appearances are underlined by the fact that the friar interprets this same blushing as a sign of Hero's innocence, and rightly so. Ironically, Claudio also says 'you seem to me as Dian in her orb' (54) and in this case, he should really rely on his sense of perception, although the night before that was exactly the mistake he made. A couple of lines further down, he refers to this again, when he says: 'Is this the prince? Is this the prince's brother? Is this face Hero's? Are your eyes your own?' (67/68) With the implicit claim that reality is right in front of everyone and easily perceptible, he only exposes his own error even more.

5. **How does this scene affect the love plot between Beatrice and Benedick?**
   First of all, he tries to console her and in so doing declares his love for her. Secondly, she is so distressed at this point in time that she has no strength to conceal her love for him anymore. Thirdly, he takes her seriously and trusts her belief in Hero's innocence. Fourthly, Beatrice is outraged that she cannot do anything to restore Hero's honour simply because she is a woman and is not able to challenge Claudio. Benedick, as a true Romantic hero, rises to the occasion by promising to do it for her. The sacrifice he would have to make by turning against his friend proves to Beatrice that he really is in love with her.

6. **During her dialogue with Benedick, Beatrice is upset on Hero's behalf and angry at Claudio but she also seems angry and frustrated with herself – why is that?**
As self-confident as Beatrice has been so far and as independent as she would like to believe herself to be, she now has to realise that much of it is an illusion. Although she pointed out several times that she does not have to marry someone who has been chosen for her and that she would prefer to remain unmarried forever, in order to avoid becoming the property of anyone, she is now faced with a situation that shows her the limits of her independence. She is deeply sorry for Hero and outraged at Claudio's behaviour but there is nothing she can do. She cannot challenge Claudio and she cannot restore Hero's reputation because after all she is a woman in a man's world. Thus, she is powerless and that upsets her even more, for she fancied herself to play an individual role in the society around her. She has to find, however, that without a man at her side who can do the things she cannot because she is a woman, she is quite helpless and in a way just as exposed to male power as Hero herself.

7. **When reading Shakespeare's plays, we make a distinction between prose and verse. Usually, one can say that Shakespeare tends to use more verse for the tragedies and includes more prose in the comedies. Particularly, in ADO, most of the speeches are composed in prose (see Glossary for 'blank verse'). Scene 4.1., however, stands out from the rest of the play, because it contains more verse than prose. Read the scene again and pay attention to the differences in style: when do people speak prose, when verse? Structure the scene accordingly and try to find out why Shakespeare might have composed it this way.**
1–21: prose
22–250: verse (except for Benedick's lines)
251–325: prose
The distinction he makes between prose and verse underlines the dramatic structure of the scene. At the beginning of the scene when the atmosphere is still light according to the impending wedding ceremony, everybody speaks prose. The changing mood is introduced with Claudio's 'Stand thee by, friar: father, by your leave,/Will you with free and unconstrained soul/Give me this maid your daughter?' (4.1.21–23) The formality of his speech signifies the seriousness of the following situation. One might assume that especially Claudio, Pedro and Leonato speak verse during this part of the scene, because it is most suitable to express their anger and grief, as well as the tragic aspect of the scene in general. Therefore, all characters speak blank verse until the next change in the stage society where only Beatrice and Benedick are left alone on stage. This change in the stage society creates a more intimate mood, especially since these two characters are in love with each other. Thus, they easily switch back into prose according to the situation they are in and the affections they have for each other.

Act 4 Scene 2

Solutions

Activities p. 76

1. **Why is it a little unusual that Dogberry would address Conrade with 'sirrah' and how does the latter react to that?**
'Sirrah' was a customary way to address servants and although Conrade might be a villain, he is still of higher social status than Dogberry is. After all, he is a follower of the Governor of Messina's brother and Dogberry is only a constable. Conrade is aware of this difference in rank and hence the impropriety of Dogberry's address,

which is why he answers: 'I am a gentleman, sir, and my name is Conrade.' (12) By addressing Dogberry as 'sir' he tries to underline the point he makes, which, however, is completely lost on Dogberry.

2. **What is Dogberry's role in the proceedings in court and how does he perceive himself?**
The role he actually plays and the role he believes he plays are very different from each other. While he believes that he is completely in control of the situation and considers himself the highest authority, whose task it is to clear up the conflict and charge the villains, in actual fact he does little in order to fulfill this role. More than revealing the villainy, he actually creates confusion and is completely lost in the moment of feeling important. The many malapropisms, which are supposed to give him a dignified style, only underline how unsuitable he is for this job.

3. **There is a lot of confusion during the examination, which makes this scene very funny. Try to act it yourselves and decide which moments are funniest.**
Free activity

Reviewing Act Four

Solutions

Activities p. 77

1. **In the 2005 BBC 'Shakespeare Retold'-production Hero's father Leonard does not doubt her innocence for a second, stays loyal to her throughout and is furious at Claude. Why do you think they changed the character's behaviour so rapidly?**
Obviously, a father behaving like Leonato in 21st-century England would be a grave anachronism, since the role of women in society and hence the relationship between father and daughter has changed so fundamentally since the Elizabethan Age. However, the emphasis must here be on the fact that the contemporary production is set in England, for in various other cultures and countries the perception of pre-marital sex and patriarchal authority does not differ all that much from Elizabethan times.

2. **Similarly, not only does her father try to defend her, but more importantly the character of Hero in the 2005 production defends herself, verbally and physically attacking the character of Don John. Additionally, she does not forgive him and turns him down when he asks her to be with him again. Try to sum up why that is and how the picture and role of women has changed between 1599 and 2005.**
The 21st century gives Hero the opportunity to do exactly what a modern reader would like her to do when reading the Shakespearean play. Since women are in fact independent now and are not subordinated to fathers or husbands, they can fully defend themselves, just as much as Beatrice would like to do but cannot. The fact that Hero in Shakespeare's play marries Claudio in the end without even so much as receiving an apology from him personally is difficult to comprehend for the modern reader and in the BBC production they have displayed the a 'normal' reaction of a 21st-century woman.

3. **Act 4 consists of only two scenes, which are very different from each other – why do you think that especially these two scenes constitute this act?**
Traditionally, the fourth act represents a turning-point of events and the first scene of act 4 in this play represents exactly that. The plot takes a profound turn and the happy ending is not as immediately conceivable as before. However, ADO is still supposed to be a comedy and the previous scene has caused distress among the characters and therefore also among the audience. In order for them to be able to carry on enjoying the play, they need a rather light interval and Dogberry and the

watch are a perfect digression. Secondly, the scene points to the overall development of the play: obviously, it will continue as a comedy, not as a tragedy. Thirdly, since two of the three villains, Borachio and Conrade, are questioned now, an important step is being taken towards the resolution of the conflict. Especially the end of the scene, when Sexton gives orders for the villains to be brought to Leonato's house, we can expect and hope for a happy ending.

4. **The first scene of act 4 is very significant when it comes to the character of Claudio. Having read this act, how would you characterise him?**
   While before, Claudio mostly seemed young and naïve, he now displays a rather cruel side of his character. The treatment of Hero is very severe indeed, considering that he claimed to be in love with her beforehand. Moreover, he makes it very obvious how easily but also profoundly he has been deceived and thus displays a tendency to be too prone to other people's influence.

5. **Think about how differently Hero's behaviour is perceived in scene 1. Who thinks what and for what reasons?**
   The reactions to Hero's blushing are very significant in context with the rest of the play. One and the same reaction, which manifests itself in outward appearance, can be perceived completely differently by the people present. While Claudio instantly believes it to be a sign of her guilt, the friar shows the same immediacy in believing it to be a sign of her innocence. Her blushing thus functions as one of the key elements in the play, for it displays how deceptive appearances can be on the one hand, but also how much true insight a person can have. At the same time, Beatrice does not react to Hero's blush at all, for she knows her to be innocent and is never shaken in her belief. In her complete trust, she does not need to perceive anything about Hero, whether positively or negatively. She simply believes in her.

6. **What is Friar Francis's function in the play and why is this function not served by a member of the main stage society?**
   He is the one who interprets Hero's reaction in the right way and thus eventually helps restore her good reputation. The only other person who has got as much insight is Beatrice, but she is a woman and therefore she cannot serve this function. All the other members of the stage society are biased and thus cannot provide the necessary neutrality.

7. **In scene 1, there are many references to eyesight – what are their functions and how does this correspond with the rest of the play?**
   All those references are of course used metaphorically to underline the main problem of the play: the unreliability of one's perceptions. Throughout the play, people refer to seeing something very clearly, while most of them experience problems with seeing what is right in front of them. Again, Beatrice is an exception. When she mockingly says in act 2 'I have a good eye, uncle, I can see a church by daylight.' (2.1.67) she is actually right, although she is joking. She does have a good eye and manages to see through all deceptions, unlike all of the others, who are blinded by their beliefs.

8. **Due to the conflict which has arisen, the stage society has split up into two opposed parties – who sides with whom and what kind of groups arise from that?**
   The events in the scene trigger important divergent dynamics in the stage society. On the one hand, Benedick changes sides out of love for Beatrice and is from now on part of the group centered around the household of Messina. Thus, the opposition between the groups is blurred, which leads to a shift of the so far prevalent stereotypes and is an important indicator for the happy ending. Secondly, the appalling behaviour Claudio and Pedro display is further emphasised by the fact that they

now belong to the group of Don John and thus present themselves as villains by association.

9. In this act, severe differences between men and women are displayed – what are they and why is this so important for the play's plot?

Through the events at church, the stereotypical roles of men and women are emphasised. The men display their power and the focus is on Hero as the property of her father. Her objectification is underlined by Claudio's rejecting her as if she were spoiled goods. Secondly, the cliché of the adulteress, so frequently referred to in the beginning of the play, seems confirmed or, at least, is alluded to again. Thus, the men (apart from Benedick) gather on one side, fully convinced of their prejudices, and the women, united in their powerlessness gather on the other. Hero seems to have lost the only object in her power, her virginity, wherefore she is more the victim of objectification than ever before.

10. Do you think, Beatrice seriously wants Benedick to kill Claudio (4.1.283)? Re-enact the dialogue between the two and try different versions of Beatrice's line?

In this moment of rage, sadness and fear, she probably does want him to kill the man who has slandered and rejected her cousin. She has been portrayed as passionate so far and thus her anger probably gets the better of her in this scene. However, she cannot seriously expect Benedick to do this for her

11. Although Hero is the main victim of Don John's scheme, Beatrice is also severely disturbed. Think about all that has happened to her since the beginning of the play. Summarise Beatrice's story up to this point and then decide whether it is justified for her to be emotionally disturbed or not.

In the first act, she sees and talks to a man who probably broke her heart. They banter and nothing much has changed. Her cousin gets engaged and although Beatrice always protests against marrying, she still seems a little concerned that she will never find a husband. At the same time, the companionship she had with Hero is now disturbed. Then she hears that Benedick, despite all her beliefs, is in love with her and now she is faced with the fact that she loves him too. All of these events and the unresolved situation with Benedick in combination with the tragic events around Hero very justly cause great distress on her side.

Worksheet 6

After the stage-society has been completed (with the exception of Friar Francis) here is a diagram showing the characters with the numbers of speeches and lines[1] they have to perform during the play. Now have a look at the stage directions announcing entrances throughout the play and tick the boxes of those scenes in which the corresponding characters actually appear.

Character	Speeches	Lines	1.1, 254	1.2, 21	1.3, 55	2.1, 293	2.2, 42	2.3, 100	3.1, 116	3.2, 100	3.3, 147	3.4, 74	3.5, 51	4.1, 316	4.2, 71	5.1, 294	5.2, 79	5.3, 33	5.4, 120
Leonato	120	350																	
Antonio	23	57																	
Hero	44	134																	
Beatrice	106	298																	
Margaret	26	57																	
Ursula	19	50																	
Friar	16	84																	
Don Pedro	134	366																	
Don John	41	121																	
Claudio	125	288																	
Benedick	134	464																	
Borachio	43	139																	
Conrade	22	39																	
Messenger	17	34																	
Balthasar	6	25																	
Boy	2	2																	
Dogberry	52	185																	
Verges	18	29																	
Sexton	7	16																	
Watch 1	4	10																	
Watch 2	16	30																	
Seacoal	10	12																	

[1] Numbers of lines according to Marvin Spevack, *The Harvard Concordance to Shakespeare, Vol. III*, based on The Riverside Shakespeare, ed. G. Blakemore Evans, Boston 1974

Worksheet 6 Solution

Character	Speeches	Lines	1.1, 254	1.2, 21	1.3, 55	2.1, 293	2.2, 42	2.3, 100	3.1, 116	3.2, 100	3.3, 147	3.4, 74	3.5, 51	4.1, 316	4.2, 71	5.1, 294	5.2, 79	5.3, 33	5.4, 120
Leonato	120	350	X	X		XX		X		X			X	X		XX			X
Antonio	23	57		X		XX										XX			XX
Hero	44	134	X			XX			X			X		X					XX
Beatrice	106	298	X			XX		X	X			X		X			X		X
Margaret	26	57				X			X			X					X		XX
Ursula	19	50				X			X			XX					X		XX
Friar	16	84												X					X
Don Pedro	134	366	X			XX		X		X				X		X		X	X
Don John	41	121	X		X	X	X			X				X					
Claudio	125	288	X			XX		X						X		X		X	X
Benedick	134	464	X			XX		X		X				X		X	X	X	X
Borachio	43	139			X	X	X				X				X	X			
Conrade	22	39			X											X			
Messenger	17	34	X			X		X					X			X			X
Balthasar	6	25	X																
Boy	2	2							X										
Dogberry	52	185									X		X		X	X			
Verges	18	29									X		X		X	X			
Sexton	7	16									X				X	X			
Watch 1	4	10									X				X	X			
Watch 2	16	30									X				X	X			
Seacoal	10	12									X								

The resulting diagram (printed above including solutions) may serve as a basis for a drama group planning a performance of ADO. In case you prefer to produce a selection of passages: which scenes would you consider to be most suitable for an amateur drama group? Give reasons in catch phrases.

Discuss which members of your group could play which roles. Remember that in Shakespeare's Globe there were no female actors. Could you imagine to attribute female parts to male actors and vice versa? Discuss.

Worksheet 6 Solution

Possible scenes for an amateur production of ADO:

1.1: Providing initial information; comic dialogues; 'merry war'

2.1: Masks; banter; music; dancing

2.3: Play within; comedy of situation; benevolent schemers and their victim; soliloquies; asides

3.1: A female version of 2.3

3.3: Farcical; clownish dialogues

4.1: Melodrama; despair; sympathy; solidarity; love

5.4: Masks; happy ending; kisses; dancing.

Act Five

Unterrichtsempfehlungen

Der letzte Akt, der in einer Komödie traditionell die Lösung aller Probleme sowie eine oder mehrere Eheschließungen bringt, ist im vorliegenden Fall mit vier Szenen und 545 Zeilen überdurchschnittlich umfangreich und sollte zügig behandelt werden, um die Freude an Shakespeare nicht zu übersättigen.
Die erste Phase der mit 304 Zeilen besonders langen Szene 5.1 mit den bitteren – fast körperlichen – Angriffen der alten Herren Leonato und Antonio auf die kraftstrotzenden Krieger Don Pedro und Claudio kann je nach Darstellung tragisch oder komisch wirken. Ähnlich ambivalent erscheinen die nachfolgende Konfrontation Benedicks mit seinen soldatischen Ex-Freunden (hier kann Worksheet No. 7 zum Einsatz kommen) sowie das anschließende reuevolle Geständnis Borachios in Anwesenheit der farcenhaften Ordnungshüter.
Auch das Ende der Szene mischt bitterste Ironie – „I thank you, princes, for my daughter's death" (244) – mit einer neuerlichen List Leonatos (255 ff.), die das *happy ending* nah erscheinen lässt. Eine kompakte inhaltliche Zusammenfassung, eventuell in Verbindung mit medialer Präsentation der Szene, kann auch zu einer Diskussion der skizzierten Ambivalenzen führen.
Die Interpretation der durchaus komischen Szene 5.2 könnte mit einem Kurzreferat über *courtly love* eingeleitet werden, da dieses Phänomen hier kräftigst parodiert und ironisiert wird, angefangen von Benedicks verzweifelten Versuchen auf dem Gebiet der Liebeslyrik bis zu seinem eher antiklimaktischen „I will live in thy heart, die in thy lap, and be buried in thy eyes: and moreover, I will go with thee to thy uncle's" (85 f.) Die Begriffe *irony* und *parody* könnten eventuell vertiefend erörtert und mit weiteren Beispielen belegt werden.
Die kurze Zwischenszene 5.3 stellt eine in manchen Augen befremdlich wirkende Parodie auf eine Totenehrung dar. Schwächere Schüler könnten sich hier zu Reimschemen und Versmaß äußern, leistungsstärkere zur Problematik einer solchen Szene in einer Komödie sowie zum merkwürdigen Verhalten Claudios insgesamt; in Stichworten: schwärmerisches Werben um gutsituierte Gouverneurstochter, brutales Verstoßen der Braut nach deren scheinbarem Fehltritt ohne Überprüfung zweifelhafter Indizien, heuchlerisches Erscheinen zur Trauungszeremonie, um dieselbe melodramatisch platzen zu lassen, Vorsatz, unmittelbar nach extrem kurzer Trauer das nächste Heiratsangebot ohne weitere Prüfung „... were she an Ethiop" (5.4, 38) – anzunehmen. Auf noch höherem Niveau könnte die grundsätzliche Diskrepanz zwischen Konventionen der Gattung Komödie und der Lebenswirklichkeit thematisiert werden.
Die letzte Szene (5.4) bringt nach nochmaligem Maskenspiel das ersehnte *happy ending* mit doppeltem Ehebeschluss. Die einschlägigen Videoproduktionen unterstreichen den Ausklang mit traditionellen Symbolen der Harmonie: Musik und Tanz.
Abschließende Diskussionen – im Plenum oder in Gruppen, die dann ihre Ergebnisse zusammentragen – könnten u. a. thematisieren, inwiefern Benedicks Dictum „man is a giddy thing" (5.4, 104) als Motto der ganzen Komödie dienen darf, ob Don Pedro seinen Ratschlag „get thee a wife, get thee a wife" (117) beherzigen sollte und wie es um die *sustainability* der beschlossenen Ehen bestellt sein mag. Im Rahmen dieser abschließenden Überlegungen können Worksheets No. 8 und 9 zum Resümee des Stückes beitragen.

Act 5 Scene 1

Solutions

Activities p. 86

1. **Analyse the dialogue between Don Leonato and Don Antonio at the beginning of the scene. What is Don Antonio's advice and how does Leonato react to it?**
Antonio tries to point out to Leonato that excessive grief will not help him in overcoming the situation. He should be moderate in his emotional reaction first of all in order not to wear himself out and secondly, because it will not help him in resolving the conflict. Leonato, however, will not hear him. First of all, he claims that his grief is extraordinary because no father ever loved his child as much as he loved Hero and that no man was ever as disappointed by his daughter. Secondly, he claims that no man could endure such grief stoically. Thirdly, he refers to the fact that a third party can always very well advise on something they are not themselves involved in. He complains that everyone who is not involved will always have something wise to say about a situation like the one at hand but that they will never be as calm once they are concerned themselves. Not even philosophers, who are supposed to be most rational, would endure pain such as his calmly. When Antonio cannot convince Leonato to endure his grief less passionately, he at least tries to turn his brother's anger on the men who are responsible for it: Claudio and Don Pedro.

2. **Judging from his first long speech and thinking back to his behaviour at the wedding, how would you characterise Leonato?**
Not only did Don Leonato side with the people who slandered his daughter, he now almost drowns in self-pity. All he can think about is his loss and his disgrace, Hero's feelings do not seem to matter to him.

3. **In the same speech, Leonato makes several comments on mankind in general – what are those? Do you think they are still true today?**
'No, no, 'tis all men's office, to speak patience/To those that wring under the load of sorrow,/But no man's virtue nor sufficiency/To be so moral, when he shall endure/The like himself [...].' (27–31) On the one hand people always know better and try to spread their good advice but when it comes to receiving advice, they believe that nobody can even understand their situation.

4. **When Claudio and Don Pedro try to take their leave of Don Leonato, they hear for the first time that Hero is supposedly dead. What do you think of their reaction?**
Leonato says: 'Thy slander hath gone through and through her heart,/And she lies buried with her ancestor: /Oh in a tomb where never scandal slept,/Save this of hers, framed by thy villainy.' (68–71) All that Claudio hears in these sentences is 'thy villainy', for that is all he comments on: 'My villainy?' (72) Clearly, the intonation of the sentence should be so that 'my' is stressed. He believes himself to be in the right and thus is not shocked and feels no repentance at Hero's death. No matter whether he is right or not, his reaction certainly seems very cold. Regardless of the fact that he believes Hero has betrayed him, if he had truly loved her before, he must feel some remorse for the fact that she is dead now. Such a sentiment is not traceable here though. He is even capable of mocking Leonato and Antonio: 'We had liked to have had our two noses snapped off with two old men without teeth.' (112/113)

5. **How do Don Pedro and Claudio react to Benedick's challenge?**
Despite the severity of the situation they do not take him seriously, they mock him even. Although they are friends and they should consider why he is not on their side in this conflict, they merely believe his challenge to be a joke and take his appearance as an opportunity to mock him about Beatrice with total disregard to the previous seriousness of the situation.

6. **Before Claudio first entered the stage in act 1, scene 1, he was described as a war hero, 'doing in the figure of a lamb the feats of a lion' – compare this statement to his behaviour in this scene.**
   First of all, the fact that Claudio simply won't take Benedick seriously, underlines his youth and inconsiderateness. However, it was suggested that he is a great soldier and very courageous, thus it is a little surprising that he does not even consider taking up the challenge. Since this is a question of honour, he should be more willing to take the challenge seriously.

Act 5 Scene 2

Solutions

Activities p. 90

1. **In Benedick's soliloquy he refers to the stereotypical man in love, who sings songs and writes poetry, which he, as a soldier, cannot do. Does that mean that he loves Beatrice less?**
   Here, as elsewhere in Shakespeare, there is implicit criticism of courtly lovers. The expression of love in songs or poetry is commonplace in Shakespeare, which indicates that this is not real love. Benedick feels inadequate because he knows the cliché and cannot live up to it but of course this means that he is truly in love. The most moving statement of his speech is when he claims that those courtly lovers 'were never so truly turned over and over as my poor self in love ...' (29/30) Clearly, he is truly in love with her, unlike those courtly lovers who are in love with declaring love in songs and poems, rather than an actual person.

2. **The scene begins with a flirt between Margaret and Benedick and carries on with a flirt between Beatrice and him. What's the main difference between the two?**
   While Benedick flirts with Margaret, it is perfectly clear that she flirts more with him. She is more aggressive, especially since she does not only use many sexual allusions ('To have no man come over me ...' [7], etc.) but also because she refers to her inferior social status. Although there are many parallels between her and Beatrice (Benedick here points out her wittiness again [9]), her status is the first thing which makes it impossible for her to trade places with Beatrice and marry a man like Benedick, and she knows that. She may flirt with him and be as witty as she can but she would never replace Beatrice. The conversation between Beatrice and Benedick is, though still witty and flirtatious, a lot calmer because there is the underlying mutual understanding that they love each other.

3. **This is the first conversation Beatrice and Benedick have since they admitted their feelings for one another. Can you detect any change in the way they speak to each other?**
   During this conversation they still mock each other and especially Beatrice tries to disagree with Benedick as much as she possibly can but all in all, the flirtatious aspect of their banter is now much stronger and the hostility is gone. When Benedick asks her why she fell in love with him (50/51), she still mocks him but never denies it and her counter-question of why he fell in love with her, underlines their mutual understanding (54–56).

4. **'Thou and I are too wise to woo peaceably.' What does Benedick mean by this?**
   By singling them out from the rest of the world more or less, Benedick strengthens the growing bond between them. He flatters both himself and Beatrice into thinking that they are superior to others because they are too realistic to be romantic and will therefore never make any foolish mistakes. Both of them are too clever to fall in love

with someone just because they are beautiful, they both prefer someone who is equally intelligent, so that they have actually something to talk about. This self-confidence in their superiority to others, however, makes it more difficult for both of them to yield and admit that they are in love.

Act 5 Scene 3

Solutions

Activities p. 91

1. **The scene begins at night and ends in the early morning, thus it begins in darkness and ends in lightness – in which way is this symbolically important for its function in the play?**
   After the many turns in ADO between tragedy and comedy, dark and light scenes, this is the final turn towards comedy. With the rising sun at the end of Scene 3, the whole play turns out to be a comedy and all tragic elements lie behind.

2. **From the original Shakespeare text, we cannot be sure in this scene who speaks which lines. Consider lines 22/23: how credible do you think it is that the Lord speaks them?**
   It is a little hard to imagine that this Lord, who has had no function in this play so far, should actually vow to visit Hero's grave once a year to pay his respects. It is far more likely that Claudio would take such a vow in order to make his repentance more significant. If he did speak these lines, however, that would mean that he doesn't sing the song. But since he did not actually woo Hero himself, it would not be totally out of character for him if he did not mourn her himself.

3. **How sad do you picture Claudio to be in this scene? Re-enact the ritual and try different versions of Claudio's behaviour.**
   Free activity

Act 5 Scene 4

Solutions

Activities p. 97

1. **Although Leonato here refers to Margaret's role in the course of events, she is let off the hook. She is even present in the scene but does not speak or comment on this, which is a little out of character. How would you explain this?**
   Most probably, the lacking resolution of Margaret's role in the scheme is due to dramatic purposes. The play must conclude soon and that requires several resolutions: Hero must come back to life so that she and Claudio can get married. Don John must be found and punished and Beatrice and Benedick must finally get together officially and be married too. Since all of this requires quite a long last scene, Margaret's function in the scheme and the question of her guilt must be more or less ignored.

2. **When Don Pedro and Claudio enter they see Benedick for the first time since act 5, scene 1. Look back at the scene. How did they leave things there and how do they talk to each other now? What do you think of this?**
   The last time they saw each other, Benedick challenged Claudio and they left each other on less than friendly terms. Claudio had a little bit of trouble believing that Benedick could actually be serious, but their formerly close friendship was definitely

disturbed. Now, the tone is jesting again and Claudio seems to be mocking Benedick about marriage just like before, which is a little unbelievable. However, first of all, their tone might be sharper than usual. Secondly, Benedick is, according to Don Pedro's description of the expression on his face, certainly still distanced and reserved. Thirdly, since the play is on the way to ending happily, all conflicts must be resolved quite quickly.

3. **What do you think of Claudio's and Hero's wedding? Why does she take him as her husband despite his previous behaviour and why is he willing to marry a woman whose face he cannot even see before the wedding?**
   In the 2005 BBC-production 'Shakespeare Retold' Hero resists all apologies and reconciliation attempts coming from Claudio, although it is hinted at a final happy ending between them when they all get together for Beatrice and Benedick's wedding five years later. From a modern perspective it is simply very difficult to understand how Hero could still marry Claudio despite what he did to her. Similarly, Claudio's behaviour of marrying a bride he believes never to have seen before is equally difficult to understand from our point of view. It is, however, perfectly in line with the character Shakespeare created, who seems to be more like a puppet than an actual individual. He falls in love too quickly, does not woo for himself, is too easily deceived and almost throughout the entire play, he is led by others rather than acting himself.

4. **Beatrice and Benedick have been in love with each other for quite a while now and both have admitted it more or less openly to each other – still, when it comes to their happy ending now, they cannot stop arguing and claiming their indifference. What are the reasons for this?**
   In line with their personalities they both try to keep the upper hand to the very last moment. Nobody wants to give in first, especially not in front of other people. At the same time, their final banter also serves dramatic purposes in closing the play according to the predominant mood of the 'merry war.'

5. **When Beatrice and Benedick finally get together, it is with his line 'Peace I will stop your mouth' and supposedly a kiss (which is how many productions stage this scene). In fact, Beatrice does not speak another line – why do you think that is?**
   Unfortunately, when Benedick claims to stop her mouth, he does so indeed, for she is silent for the rest of the play. One could interpret this as an indication that now that she will marry, she cannot keep up her independent and willful behaviour anymore, because that is not the proper behaviour for a wife. In that case, one could have more than reasonable doubts whether this marriage will go well. However, reading Shakespeare more positively, the reasons for her silence might just be that dramatically this plotline is brought to an end and therefore any contribution from her side is not needed anymore. The rest of the scene includes a last presentation of Benedick's wit, he and Claudio finally make up and Don John has been found. Thus, the play can end, according to the rules of comedy, with two marriages and Beatrice's character thus fades into the background.

6. **Claudio's final statement indicates that Benedick will cheat on Beatrice, as soon as he gets the chance. Do you think that's true?**
   Most probably not. Now that he has finally agreed to marry after years of being against it, it is not very likely that he will cheat on Beatrice. Claudio's statement rather reflects one of the predominant themes of the play, adultery, only that now it is applied to men, rather than women.

Reviewing Act Five

Solutions

Activities p. 98

1. **Similar to act 2, in act 5 masking plays a significant role. Compare the two scenes – what are the differences?**
   In act 2, the masks were a significant element to create the confusion necessary for the plotline. They represented the opposition between appearance and reality in various forms: 1. Hero and her family believe that Don Pedro woos her. 2. Claudio believes that Don Pedro betrays him by wooing Hero for himself. 3. Don John gets his first chance to cause mischief. 4. The men and women are generally uncertain of who it is they dance with, which is characteristic of Don John's later scheme. 5. Beatrice takes the opportunity to scold Benedick, pretending to be unaware of her dance partner's real identity. 6. Benedick has to listen to what he believes is Beatrice's real opinion of him.
   In act 5, the masks' function is the opposite one: they function as first a disguise and then a revealing of the truth, whereas in act 2 they are a means of conveying wrong truths. After the final revelation in act 5, when the women take their masks off, one can be sure that that which is presented now, is the final truth. Thus, the play can end happily because finally, the opposition between appearance and reality is overcome and things appear as they really are.

2. **In the final act, all conflicts are resolved, and in the end almost everyone is happy. Recapitulate the events of the play – which things had to happen in order to ensure the happy ending?**
   Hero's honour had to be restored, i.e. first Leonato had to understand that she is innocent, then Don Pedro and Claudio.
   Claudio had to repent his treatment of Hero and show his maturity by making 'reasonable' decisions, such as promising Leonato to marry his supposed niece.
   Benedick had to prove to Beatrice not only that he loves her but also that he is loyal to her and would not, as before, disappoint her, which he made clear by challenging Claudio on Hero's behalf.
   Beatrice had to overcome her pride and self-righteousness in order to be finally happy with Benedick.
   Don John and his companions had to be found out and punished.
   It had to be revealed to Claudio that Hero is still alive and still willing to marry him.
   Benedick had to overcome his dislike of marriage and be willing to give up his bachelorhood despite the danger of turning into a cuckold.

3. **Claudio's reaction to Hero's coming back to life and standing in front of him to be married to him is merely 'Another Hero?' (5.4.62). In order to believe that he really loves her and wants to marry her, there must be another nonverbal reaction. Describe how you would play this as an actress/actor.**
   There are basically two ways of staging this, depending on the view one takes of Claudio. If he is seen as the likeable, romantic, young man, he must compensate the lack of verbal reaction by his non-verbal behaviour towards Hero, such as taking her into his arms, kissing her, taking long looks at her and holding on to her for the rest of scene; after all, she is what he claimed to be the love of his life and all of a sudden she has risen from the dead, which requires an appropriately emotional reaction.
   On the other hand, considering his rashness in falling in love with her as well as discarding her as a whore, it is possible to portray him quite negatively. In this case he might not care whom he marries and in that case he might be surprised but not necessarily very moved by Hero's return.

4. Analyse Beatrice and Benedick's final dialogue – how do they finally end up together?

The final dialogue is characteristic of the two characters who are both equally afraid to give up their superiority and show weaknesses. The similarity of their characters is echoed in the dialogue where they are equally precautious. Instead of declaring their love, they both ask the other 'Do not you love me?' (74/77) and instead of admitting it, they refer back to other people's opinions: '... they swore you did.'/'they did swear you did.' (76/79) Despite their reluctance to admit their feelings, the parallelisms of the dialogue create a new unity between them that undoubtedly creates the mood for a final happy ending ('They swore that you were almost sick for me.' - 'They swore that you were wellnigh dead for me.' 80/81). Characteristically, it is Claudio's and Hero's interference that helps them out of their situation, since due to their insistence, both Beatrice and Benedick simply have to yield instead of taking action: '... here's our hands against our hearts ... I take thee for pity.' (91/92) says Benedick, and Beatrice, still stubborn, pretends that this is still against her will: 'I yield upon great persuasion, and partly to save your life, for I was told, you were in a consumption.' (93–95)

Reviewing the Play

Solutions

Activities p. 98

1. If you were asked to play a part in ADO, which role would you choose? Justify your choice.

Students usually pick Beatrice and Benedick, because of their funny dialogues and because they are after all the central characters – more so than Hero and Claudio.

2. Find and describe as many eavesdropping episodes as you can and analyse their function within the plot.

The first two eavesdropping scenes happen offstage. The information conveyed through these sets the plot in motion: the impending marriage and Don John's evil plan. The next two eavesdropping scenes are part of the scheme laid out for Benedick and Beatrice and their central function within the play is to bring the couple together. Furthermore, these scenes create comedy, since the audience feels superior due to their insight and the behaviour of both Beatrice and Benedick has great comic potential.

3. Which of the two marriages looks more promising: Claudio and Hero or Benedick and Beatrice? Take into consideration the behaviour of the four characters during the play.

As much as Beatrice and Benedick's relationship is characterised by aggression and opposition, their love seems much more convincing than Claudio and Hero's. Hero never even expresses her love of him and Claudio falls in and out of love so easily that it is hard to imagine that their love is going to last very long. Beatrice and Benedick, on the other hand, seem to have found their match and one can imagine that despite (or because of) their continuous banter they will have a happy marriage.

4. During the Victorian age Beatrice was often judged as an odious woman, the posing, self-centered embodiment of pride, showing herself off to attract a husband. Nowadays people tend to see in her the personification of wit, liveliness and emancipation. What do you think of her?

The perception of the play is always influenced by the society of the time it is produced in. In Victorian times, the perception of what a woman ideally should be like was very different from the perception of the 21st century. The Victorians believed that a woman should be modest, shy, chaste, never speak unless spoken to, well-educated and beautiful but never intentionally drawing attention to herself. Nowadays, such a conception of an ideal woman no longer really exists, since the rules of society are not as strict as they used to be all those years ago. Secondly, today nobody expects women to subordinate themselves to the society around them and a lively, witty, intelligent woman is not so unusual anymore. Thus, from a modern perspective, Beatrice embodies a very attractive 21st-century woman and her outspokenness is something postmodernity very much approves of.

5. **Discuss the implications of the title of the comedy, remembering the pun on 'nothing' and 'noting'. Would you have chosen a different title? If so, justify your suggestion.**
The play might have been called something like 'Appearances are deceptive' but the given title is clearly the most suitable one, for it draws on the central theme of the play in two ways: first of all, there is much ado about nothing, for almost the entire plot develops according to something that never happened. Secondly, there is much ado about noting, since people believe to have seen or heard something all the time and act accordingly. The ambiguous implication of the title thus suggests in one line nearly everything this play is about.

6. **ADO has basically three different plotlines: one main plot and two subplots. Write three summaries, one for each plotline.**
Main plot: Claudio falls in love with Hero and asks Don Pedro to woo her for him. She accepts him and with the consent of her father, they get engaged. The villain Don John makes Claudio believe that Hero has been unfaithful to him, wherefore Claudio calls off the wedding in front of the whole congregation. She faints out of shock and is proclaimed dead but in actual fact, her father hides her in his house. When it turns out that she was innocent and that it was all only Don John's evil plan, Claudio repents and mourns for the dead Hero. In order to make up for his shameful behaviour, he promises Hero's father to marry his niece, who is supposed to look exactly like Hero. When they are about to be betrothed, Hero reveals her true identity and the two are happily united.
Sub-plot no. 1: Beatrice and Benedick both share their dislike of each other as well as of marriage. Since this seems to make them the perfect match, the society of Messina lays out a scheme to bring them together. They are both told that the respective other is in love with them and thus they fall in love too. When Claudio refuses to marry Hero, Beatrice is very distressed and Benedick steps in to console and help her, which gives them both the chance to declare their love for each other. After everything has been resolved and Claudio and Hero are reunited, Benedick proposes to Beatrice too and after their usual banter, she accepts him and they get married in the end.
Sub-plot 2: The watch of Messina, led by the constable Dogberry, overhear a conversation between the villains, where they talk about the scheme they have laid out to ruin Claudio's and Hero's happiness. The watch arrest them and charge them at court. There the whole story is revealed, which is reported back to Leonato and thus Hero's honour is restored.

7. **One of the major themes of ADO is the opposition between appearance and reality. Make two lists: one of the incidents where people *believe* something and one where people *know* something. How do these incidents influence the main plot?**

Don Antonio and Don Leonato believe that Don Pedro wants to marry Hero	Don John and his companions know that Claudio wants to marry Hero
Claudio believes that Don Pedro wants to woo Hero for himself	Beatrice knows that Benedick is behind the mask and takes the opportunity to mock him
Benedick believes that Beatrice is in love with him	Beatrice knows that Hero is innocent
Beatrice believes that Benedick is in love with her	
Claudio believes that Hero has been unfaithful to him	
Don Leonato believes Hero to be guilty	
Friar Francis believes that Hero is innocent	
Claudio and Don Pedro believe Hero to be dead	

8. An important aspect of ADO is the 'merry war' between Beatrice and Benedick. Another famous commonplace is the phrase 'All is fair in love and war' by Francis Edward Smedley, an English novelist of the nineteenth century. How does Shakespeare combine the two phenomena love and war in his play? And do you think that all is fair in love and war?

War serves as the background of the play, for the action begins immediately after battle has ceased and the men arriving at Messina are all soldiers. Thus, the war metaphor can be found throughout the play, especially when Beatrice and Benedick are concerned. Shakespeare makes use of the metaphor to emphasise the violence of love but also the passion that exists between these two characters. The assumption is that both realms of life, love and war, are free from moral restraint and that one blow is answered by the next, which is indeed what Beatrice and Benedick do. They swerve between attack and retreat and the dialogues they have closely resemble actual duels. The second question is liable to various answers.

9. When you think of the eight central characters of the play, certain parallels become obvious. Which can you identify? Activities p. 99

Similar social structure: Don Leonato – Hero – Beatrice/Don Pedro – Claudio – Benedick. Respective couples Hero – Claudio/Beatrice – Benedick. Similar relationships Hero (young, naïve, guided by her father and by Beatrice) – Beatrice (older, wiser, cynical, authoritative)/Claudio (young, naïve, guided by Don Pedro and Benedick) – Benedick (older, wiser, cynical, authoritative). Brothers: Don Leonato – Don Antonio/Don Pedro – Don John. 'Servants': Borachio and Conrade – Margaret and Ursula. Margaret as the socially inferior version of Beatrice. The young ones (Hero and Claudio) untypically deceiving the older ones (Beatrice and Benedick).

10. In the 2005 BBC 'Shakespeare Retold' production, the play is set in a TV company. Beatrice and Benedick are both television presenters putting a show together and Don Leonato is the producer of the show. Can you find any reasons for the setting? Think of the opposition between appearance and reality. How does this relate to the setting?

By setting the play in and around a TV-production studio, the topos of appearance vs. reality is always present: as real as things on TV might seem, the whole concept is basically about pretending. Whatever is seen on TV should be questioned, since no medium is as good at creating illusions. There are huge discrepancies not only between reality and the things mediated by television but also between what is to be seen and what goes on behind the scenes. Especially the fact that Beatrice and Benedick present the same show together, thus have to seem like they get on really well, whereas in actual fact they hate each other, is a constant reminder to question things and not to take anything at face value. Much of the play is about information and the mediation of information, which is just what the function of TV is. Secondly, on screen things may seem very different from what they actually are behind the scenes. The 2005 Beatrice and Benedick, for instance, pretend to get on really well as soon as they are live on air and the moment the camera is switched off, they take up their argument again.

11. **Many of the metaphors in the play are inspired by the comparison between man and animal. Where can you find such animal imagery? Gather together the most important ones. Why do you think there is such an emphasis on this?**
Beatrice: her tongue is faster than Benedick's horse (1.1.113), 'harpy' (2.1.232), 'lapwing' (3.1.24), 'haggard' (3.1.36), fish (3.1.29), she speaks of her 'wild heart' that she will tame to Benedick's hand (3.1.112). She and Benedick are also the 'two bears.' (3.2.65)
Benedick: 'jade' (1.1.116), 'savage bull' (1.1.211/5.4.43), 'oyster' (2.3.21) 'kid-fox' (2.3.37), fish (2.3.101)
Claudio: 'figure of a lamb', 'feats of a lion' (1.1.12), 'poor hurt fowl' (2.1.175), a calf (5.4.50)
Hero: 'forward March chick' (1.3.45), accused of being as lusty as 'pampered animals' (4.1.57)
Margaret: 'greyhound's mouth' (5.2.9), her tongue runs 'Not a false gallop' (3.4.80)
Don John: 'trusted with a muzzle' (1.3.25) does not want to 'sing in my cage' (1.3.27)
Dogberry: 'ass' (4.2.67 ff.)
The use of all these metaphors, which seemingly underlines the difference between man and animal, in actual fact emphasises the opposite. Due to the frequent comparison it becomes clear, how irrational and animalistic human beings also are, especially when it comes to love. Falling in love has little to do with rationality, which is the most important quality that distinguishes man from animal. In ADO, however, people tend to show more animalistic traits than human traits. Moreover, the animal imagery is also related to the emphasis the play puts on Cupid. Love happens coincidentally due to Cupid's choice. His method of shooting arrows at people who are supposed to fall in love with each other makes him a hunter, which emphasises the conception of the characters as animals even more. They are hunted down by Cupid and then fall in love because they don't have a choice. The way Beatrice and Benedick show their affection for one another through their 'merry war' can be compared to a mating ritual between two animals, which is not entirely comprehensible to humans.

12. **One of Shakespeare's most famous sonnets is number 116. In the 'Shakespeare Retold' version Beatrice and Benedick interpret the sonnet together in a crucial scene towards their personal happy ending – having read the sonnet, why do you think the screenwriter chose this particular one out of the 154 that Shakespeare wrote?**
Let me not to the marriage of true minds
Admit impediments. Love is not love
Which alters when it alteration finds,
Or bends with the remover to remove:
O, no! it is an ever-fixed mark,
That looks on tempests and is never shaken;
It is the star to every wandering bark,

Whose worth's unknown, although his height be taken.
Love's not Time's fool, though rosy lips and cheeks
Within his bending sickle's compass come;
Love alters not with his brief hours and weeks,
But bears it out even to the edge of doom.
    If this be error and upon me proved,
    I never writ, nor no man ever loved.

Since the main point of the sonnet is to define what love is and what it is not, it is highly relevant to ADO. Its interpretation however, would imply that Claudio does not love Hero, because he does indeed bend 'with the remover to remove'. And his love is immediately shaken by the arising tempest. Most importantly, the first two lines echo the wedding vows usually spoken in church ('if anyone knows of any legal impediment, why this couple should not wed, step forward or forever hold thy peace'), which is brought to perversity by the wedding scene happening between Claudio and Hero. He believes to know an impediment and steps forward himself to declare it, although he is the lover himself. The speaker of the sonnet says, 'let me not to the marriage of true minds admit impediments', thus stepping away in respect of true love. The fact that in ADO the groom himself steps in just makes clear, in line with the sonnet, that this is not a marriage of true minds.
If one believes that Beatrice and Benedick have, concealed by their hostilities, loved each other all along, the third quatrain applies to their love in contrast to the one between Claudio and Hero: no matter how long it has been, their love has passed the test of time, which is a very positive outlook for their future. Particularly the line 'though rosy lips and cheeks/Within his bending sickle's compass come', points out that Beatrice and Benedick have a much better foundation for their marriage than Claudio and Hero do, since their union is only based on outward beauty, which will necessarily fade.
Another parallel between the sonnet and the play is that the sonnet's tone of voice resembles the absolute conviction that the characters in ADO show too. To claim that the statements of the three quatrains are true or otherwise no human being has ever been in love is just as strong as claiming that otherwise the speaker has not written a word, which is a *contradictio in re*, since the evidence for his writing is right in front of us. This profound conviction of something is very similar to Claudio's conviction of Hero's guilt, as well as Beatrice's conviction of her cousin's innocence.

Worksheet 7

You can see two different film versions of the same scene from ADO below. Which scene do you believe this to be and what does Benedick say to Claudio? Which version do you find more credible? Give reasons.

Worksheet 8

Below you can see a drawing by C. Walter Hodges. Which scene of ADO might be in performance here? Identify the characters on stage and write down the lines you suppose them to speak at this moment.

Worksheet 8 Solution

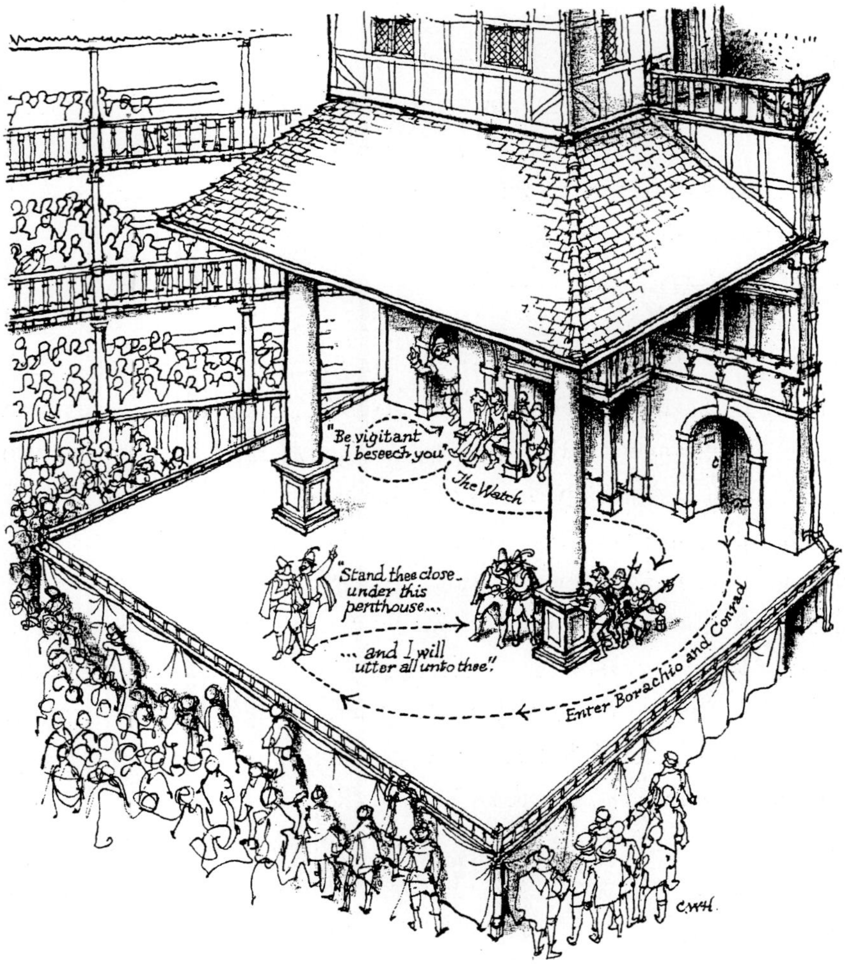

Worksheet 9

How well do you know ADO?

The society in ____________, which consists of the ____________, ________________, his brother, ______________________, his daughter, __________, and his niece, ______________, is disturbed by a group of soldiers in Act ___, Scene ___. Led by the Prince of ____________, ______________, this company includes his brother, ______________, who is a ____________, and the young soldiers, Signor ____________ and Signor ______________. When they arrive, it becomes clear that ________________ and ________________ already have a certain history, for they ____. Claudio, on the other hand, ______________________ Hero, and his mentor, Don Pedro, promises ______________________. This happens in Act ___, Scene ___, but due to the fact that ______________ has decided to cause mischief, ____________ believes for a while that ________________ has betrayed him and ____________________________________. However, this is soon cleared up. ____________ and ______________ dance together at the same time and Beatrice ________________, which greatly upsets him. However, the rest of the characters in the play decide to ________________, for they believe them to be ______________________. This romantic subplot happens mainly in scenes ____ and ____. The men deceive Benedick by claiming that ____ whilst he is __________________. The women do the same to Beatrice and talk loudly about ____________________________________, while Beatrice is ________________. The news they believe to have received, has a profound effect on Beatrice and Benedick: ____. In the meantime, preparations for the wedding between ______________________ are going on, but at the same time, ________________ forms the evil plan to ruin the marriage. He and ______________ make ____________ and ________________ believe that Hero ________________________________. When the wedding morning has arrived, ____________ shames ______ in front of the whole congregation and she seems to ______________________. Out of love for ____________, Benedick promises to ________________________ and help clear up the misunderstanding, but this is actually achieved by ______________, who makes ______________ and ______________ confess their crime. ____________, who believes Hero to be dead, promises ________________ to marry another niece of his as a means of repentance but when the wedding morning has come, it turns out that ____. Thus, the couple have found their happy ending and Beatrice and Benedick finally stop quarrelling too, so that ____.

Worksheet 9 Solution

How well do you know ADO?

The society in Messina, which consists of the Governor, Don Leonato, his brother, Don Antonio, his daughter, Hero, and his niece, Beatrice, is disturbed by a group of soldiers in Act 1, Scene 1. Led by the Prince of Arragon, Don Pedro, this company includes his brother, Don John, who is a bastard and the young soldiers, Signor Claudio and Signor Benedick. When they arrive, it becomes clear that Beatrice and Benedick already have a certain history, for they immediately start to quarrel. Claudio, on the other hand, falls in love with Hero, and his mentor, Don Pedro, promises to woo her for him. This happens in Act 2, Scene 1, but due to the fact that Don John has decided to cause mischief, Claudio believes for a while that Don Pedro has betrayed him and is in love with Hero himself. However, this is soon cleared up. Beatrice and Benedick dance together at the same time and Beatrice insults him, which greatly upsets him. However, the rest of the characters in the play decide to set them up, for they believe them to be the perfect couple. This romantic sub-plot happens mainly in scenes 2.3 and 3.1. The men deceive Benedick by claiming that Beatrice is in love with him whilst he is eavesdropping. The women do the same to Beatrice and talk loudly about Benedick's being in love with her, while Beatrice is eavesdropping. The news they believe to have received, has a profound effect on Beatrice and Benedick: they both declare right after the respective scene that they will requite the other's love. In the meantime, preparations for the wedding between Claudio and Hero are going on, but at the same time, Don John forms the evil plan to ruin the marriage. He and Borachio make Claudio and Don Pedro believe that Hero is not a virgin anymore. When the wedding morning has arrived, Claudio shames Hero in front of the whole congregation and she seems to drop dead. Out of love for Beatrice, Benedick promises to challenge Claudio and help clear up the misunderstanding, but this is actually achieved by Dogberry, who makes Borachio and Conrade confess their crime. Claudio, who believes Hero to be dead, promises Don Leonato to marry another niece of his as a means of repentance but when the wedding morning has come, it turns out that the bride is Hero herself, who is still alive. Thus, the couple have found their happy ending and Beatrice and Benedick finally stop quarrelling too, so that both couples can get married in the end.

Much Ado About Nothing as a Shakespearean Comedy

Solutions

Activities p. 101

1. **Why is *Much Ado About Nothing* usually listed among Shakespeare's comedies?**
   It contains most of the traditional elements. First of all ADO has a happy ending which includes several marriages after the respective couples have overcome the obstacles between them. Secondly, especially Beatrice and Benedick are comic characters, due to their verbal comedy which is displayed in their quarrels but also due to their function in comedy of situation as in scenes 2.3 and 3.1. These eavesdropping scenes form a crucial comic element of the play. Dogberry and his watch add a farcical element, which is used as comic relief especially after rather melodramatic scenes.

2. **Try to remember a comedy you have recently watched (theatre, film or TV). Describe parallels to ADO.**
   Any modern Romantic comedy basically follows Shakespearean comedy in the main pattern. One or more couples try to find their way towards each other throughout the course of the story. In modern Romantic comedies the respective couples are easily identifiable from the start, so that the audience only has to wait for them to get together. This involves more or less serious obstacles like misunderstandings, quarrels or another potential partner (who is usually portrayed as the 'wrong' one from the start). The other two elements, verbal comedy and comedy of situation, can also be found in any modern film. Funny dialogues between the lovers are almost always a part of modern films and comedy of situation even more so, like embarrassing moments for either of the two prospective partners or through their comic sidekicks.

3. **What is comic about Dogberry and his men?**
   The group around Dogberry resemble an element usually included in farce, rather than comedy. The verbal comedy which borders on nonsense is supported by slapstick elements, for example when they try to arrest Conrade and Borachio. Dogberry himself in his ambition to be someone greater than he is and the mismatching stupidity is highly entertaining, especially since the audience feels superior to him.

The Play within the Play

Solution

Activity p. 103

Discuss and enact some implicit 'plays within' in *Much Ado About Nothing*.
a) Have a look at *King Lear* (1.2 and 2.1) and *Othello* (4.1), explain and discuss how and why two notorious villains – Edmund and Iago – deliberately misinterpret 'plays within'.
Edmund deceives Gloucester, his father, about Edgar. He wants to destroy the reputation of Gloucester's good son in order to get his inheritance: 'Legitimate Edgar, I must have your land' (LR, 1.2.16)

Iago makes Othello watch an encounter between Cassio and Bianca. He makes him believe that Desdemona, Othello's faithful wife, has committed adultery with Cassio. To prove his story Iago uses a handkerchief, stolen from Desdemona and now in Bianca's hands. He pursues several intentions: to stir Othello's hatred and jealousy against Cassio, to destroy the reputation of Desdemona, who supposedly gave the precious handkerchief to Cassio, who passed it on to another mistress of his, Bianca. In the last resort Iago intends to drive Othello into madness, murder and suicide, all of which succeeds.

b) Explain *King Richard III* (3.7).
Richard, Duke of Gloucester, another notorious villain, and Buckingham, his accomplice, put on a show to convince the citizens of London that Richard will be an excellent and pious king, if and when chosen by the citizens. As Edmund and Iago, the villains succeed in deceiving their victims on the stage. Nevertheless, the theatre audience is expected to relish this play within as a comedy within a tragedy/history. Conclusion to be drawn from the three last examples: Misinterpreting scenes from Shakespeare may be dangerous.

Queen Elizabeth I

Solutions

Activities p. 105

1. **Compare Hero and Queen Elizabeth – what do they have in common?**
   In a sense, their most valuable property is their virginity, only that Elizabeth was able to use it to her advantage in a way, since she could hold up foreign relations by suggesting willingness to marry on her part. Both women live in a patriarchal world, which makes it difficult for them to be taken seriously, something which Hero fails to achieve throughout the play. Her marriage to Claudio in the end is as much a confirmation of patriarchal society as Elizabeth's lifelong refusal to do the same was a rejection of male domination.

2. **Compare Beatrice and Queen Elizabeth – what do they have in common?**
   Beatrice's refusal to subordinate herself to the men of her society very much resembles Elizabeth's similar attitude. In the play, Beatrice is given a certain power over herself and her decisions due to the fact that she does not seem to have parents and thus no direct superior, just as much as Elizabeth, who, as absolute monarch, only had one authority above her – God. Both women make use of their independence by refusing to marry as long as they can. Beatrice finally chooses Benedick and Elizabeth basically outgrew the age in which to get married, but both make and made the point that they would only marry whom they choose.

3. **When Claudio accuses Hero of infidelity in act 4, scene 1, he uses similar comparisons like the Elizabethan poets – which ones and what is the effect created?**
   'You seem to me as Dian in her orb,/As chaste as is the bud ere it be blown.' (4.1.54/55)
   The comparison between Diana and Elizabeth was frequently made for several reasons: her chastity, her power as huntress, her resolute treatment of men, and her unattainability as a goddess. The image was employed in love poetry, thus Claudio's use of it here ironically underlines his cruelty in rejecting her. Moreover, Shakespeare's image evokes the association with Elizabeth and the two roles she had to play as a female monarch in a nevertheless patriarchal society.

4. **Would you have liked to be Queen Elizabeth I or not? Give reasons for your opinion.**
   Free activity

Klausur

Twelfth Night, 2.5.4 – 46

The following passage is part of a scene taking place in the garden of a wealthy countess, named Olivia. Chief of staff of her household is Malvolio. In order to improve his social position, he intends to marry the countess. His chief antagonist is Maria, a female servant of Olivia's under the command of Malvolio. Maria has forged a letter in Olivia's handwriting, implying that the countess secretly adores Malvolio.
First we see three other male characters: Sir Toby, Olivia's uncle, who is mainly given to the pleasures of life, Sir Andrew, his not very intelligent companion, and Fabian, another of Olivia's servants, presently in disgrace with her for having organized a bear-beating, a cruel sport, in which a bear, chained and defenseless, was attacked by dogs.
Read the passage carefully and fulfil the ensuing tasks.

SIR TOBY Wouldst thou not be glad to have the niggardly[1] rascally sheep-biter[2] come by some notable shame?

FABIAN I would exult[3], man, You know he brought me out o' favour with my lady about a bear-baiting here.

SIR TOBY To anger him, we'll have the bear again; and we will fool him black and blue, shall we not, Sir Andrew?

SIR ANDREW And[4] we do not, it is pity of our lives.

SIR TOBY Here comes the little villain.

Enter MARIA

How now, my metal of India[5]?

MARIA Get ye all three into the box-tree[6]. Malvolio's coming down this walk. He has been yonder i'the sun practising behaviour to his own shadow this half hour. Observe him, for the love of mockery, for I know this letter will make a contemplative[7] idiot of him. Close, in the name of jesting!

The men hide

Lie thou there [*Drops a letter*]; for here comes the trout that must be caught with tickling[8].

Exit

Enter MALVOLIO

MALVOLIO 'Tis but fortune; all is fortune. Maria once told me she[9] did affect[10] me, and I have heard herself come thus near, that should she fancy[11], it should be one of my complexion[12]. Besides, she uses me with a more exalted[13] respect than any one else that follows her. What should I think on't?

1 **niggardly** mean
2 **sheep-biter** dissembler, pretender
3 **exult** rejoice
4 **And** if
5 **my metal of India** i. e. 'my gold of India', affectionate address
6 **box-tree** an evergreen hedge or tree
7 **contemplative** meditative
8 **trout ... tickling** proverbial, special method of catching fish
9 **she** i. e. Olivia
10 **affect** like
11 **fancy** fall in love
12 **complexion** looks, temperament
13 **exalted** high

Klausur

Sir Toby Here's an overweening[14] rogue!

Fabian O peace! Contemplation[15] makes a rare turkey-cock[16] of him; how he jets under his advanced plumes[17]!

Sir Andrew 'Slight[18], I could so beat the rogue!

Fabian Peace, I say!

Malvolio To be Count Malvolio!

Sir Toby Ah, rogue!

Sir Andrew Pistol him, pistol him[19]!

Fabian Peace, peace!

Malvolio There is example for't: the Lady of the Strachy married the yeoman of the wardrobe –

Sir Andrew Fie on him, Jezebel![20]

Fabian O peace! Now he's deeply in. Look how imagination blows him.

Malvolio Having been three months married to her, sitting in my state –

Sir Toby O for a stone-bow[21] to hit him in the eye!

Malvolio Calling my officers about me, in my branched[22] velvet-gown, having come from a day-bed, where I have left Olivia sleeping –

Sir Toby Fire and brimstone!

Fabian O peace, peace!

Malvolio And then to have the humour of the state[23]; and after a demure travel of regard[24] – telling them I know my place, as I would they should do theirs – to ask for my kinsman Toby –

---

14 **overweening** arrogant
15 **contemplation** thinking about himself
16 **turkey-cock** symbol of vanity
17 **jets ... plumes** goes about under his uplifted feathers
18 **'Slight** by God's light (oath)
19 **Pistol him** Shoot him
20 **Jezebel** biblical widow of king Ahab, who was so proud that she was sentenced to death by being killed and eaten by dogs
21 **stone-bow** crossbow used for shooting stones
22 **branched** ornamented with flowers
23 **humour ... state** behaviour of great authority
24 **demure ... regard** looking at them gravely

Activities

X **1. Summarise the contents of the above passage. (Comprehension)**

2. Outline structural similarities and differences with regard to ADO, 2.3. (Analysis)

x **3. To what extent does Malvolio resemble Benedick? (Comparison)**

4. In what aspects do they differ?

comments?

Klausur Solution

1. Summarise the contents of the above passage.

Lines 4–12: Sir Toby, Fabian and Sir Andrew are very much looking forward to angering an unnamed person, who is first evoked by some pretty abusive terms 'niggardly rascally sheepbiter' (4 f.) – and later turns out to be Malvolio, the Countess Olivia's steward. Fabian's chief motive seems to be revenge, as 'he brought me out o'favour with my lady about a bearbaiting here.' (6 f.) The avengers are planning to anger their enemy in much the same way as a bear was tortured in the cruel sport of bear-baiting: '... we'll have the bear again ... we will fool him black and blue ...' (8 f.). Their malicious joy is heightened by the arrival of Maria, cheerfully referred to as 'little villain ... my metal of India.' (11 f.)
13–19: Maria appears and immediately starts giving instructions to the three men, showing who 'wears the trousers'. She announces the forthcoming arrival of Malvolio, scorns his vanity – 'He has been yonder i'the sun practising behaviour to his own shadow this half hour.' (14 f.) – orders them to observe Malvolio from a hiding-place, puts a letter on the ground, which 'will make a contemplative idiot of him' (16), and disappears before Malvolio enters.
20–46: Malvolio, not at first noticing the letter, begins a long soliloquy, in which he daydreams about his imagined future position as 'Count Malvolio' (30), Olivia's husband to be. His speech is time and again commented on by the hidden spectators' furious exclamations, which remain unnoticed by the day-dreaming soliloquiser.

2. Outline structural similarities and differences with regard to ADO, 2.3.

The episode summarised above resembles scene 2.3 of *Much Ado About Nothing* in various aspects. Both episodes are clearly plays within the play. In each case there is a single victim duped by a company of schemers. In *Much Ado* the plotters perform their play and Benedick performs the part of the audience, thinking himself to be an eavesdropper, not realising that the others are putting up a show intended to dupe him and to enjoy themselves. In *Twelfth Night*, on the other hand, Malvolio, as a kind of puppet on strings, performs a play that Maria has devised for him and that he does not really know about, whereas the schemers enjoy themselves as eavesdroppers and audience at the same time.
Technically speaking the victim soliloquises, whereas the plotters engage in a dialogue. The comic effect of the whole construction is based on dramatic conventions. The soliloquies are seemingly addressed only to the speaker himself, whereas in reality they are meant to reveal his thoughts, ideas, reflections, plans, intentions, emotions etc. to the audience in the theatre. The 'asides', in both cases not marked as such, are uttered by the schemers, intended to be heard and understood by their accomplices and by the audience, but not by their victim, who is indeed closer to them on the stage than to the audience in their seats. This is called a 'convention', i. e. a kind of agreement between a dramatist and his audience, which is generally accepted although far from every day reality. Furthermore the comic effect is created by a feeling of superiority of the audience over the victim or – to put it differently – by joyful identification with the schemers against their victim.

Klausur Solution

3. To what extent does Malvolio resemble Benedick?

A common denominator between Malvolio and Benedick – at least in the opening phases of the two episodes – is their vanity, their extremely high esteem of their own persons. Benedick first amuses himself about his old friend and companion, Claudio, whom he scorns for having fallen in love, for having turned from a soldier into an intellectual: '... turned orthography, his words are a fantastical banquet ...' (ADO, 2.3.18 f.), which in Benedick's view means a downfall. He goes on to assert that no living woman could be good enough for him (Ibid., 23–30). Balthasar's music and song are later ridiculed in his 'asides': '... now is his soul ravished: is it not strange that sheep's guts hale souls out of men's bodies? (53 ff.) ... And he had been a dog that should have howled thus, they would have hanged him ... I had as lief have heard the night-raven ...' (76 ff.).

Malvolio, for his part, considers himself to be a darling of fate and of the Duchess Olivia: '... all is fortune. Maria once told me she did affect me ... it should be one of my complexion ... she uses me with a more exalted respect than any one else that follows her': (*Twelfth Night,* 5.20 ff.). Totally ignoring the furious interjections of the eavesdroppers, who are feared by the theatre audience to betray themselves, he goes on to imagine himself as 'Count Malvolio ... in my branched velvet gown, having come from a day-bed, where I have left Olivia sleeping ... telling them I know my place, as I would they should do theirs ...' (Ibid., 30–46).

4. In what aspects do they differ?

More important than the similarities are the differences between Malvolio and Benedick. Malvolio, whose name suggests that he has evil intentions, will remain an outsider who cannot be converted. His name is therefore a 'telling' or 'labelling' name. As a character he seems closer to Don John than to Benedick. This may also be deduced from his view on the Duchess Olivia. Nowhere does he mention a feeling of consideration, let alone of love for her. His one and only intention is to heighten his social position at her side and then to treat or rather mistreat everybody else from above.

Benedick, on the other hand, is converted into a real lover, although by the end of the scene he still seems somewhat conceited and declares to act out of pity: '... if I do not take pity of her I am a villain ... I will go get her picture' (ADO, 2.3.228 f.). But we know that, especially through their common sympathy for the slandered Hero, he and Beatrice become a couple of true lovers who might live happily ever after ...

Discover ...

Shakespeare-Textausgaben
Landeskundliche Themenhefte

Herausgegeben von
Klaus Hinz und Engelbert Thaler (ab 2007)

Africa – Postcolonial Experiences
Von Monika Teichmann
70 S. Best.-Nr. **978-3-14-040100-5**
Lehrerheft. Best.-Nr. **978-3-14-040101-2**

African-American Experiences – From Exploitation to Participation
Von Wiltrud Frenken, Angela Luz und Brigitte Prischtt
55 S. Best.-Nr. **978-3-14-040116-6**
Lehrerheft. Best.-Nr. **978-3-14-040117-3**

Australia and New Zealand – Neither Down nor Under
Von Rainer H. Berthelmann
95 S. Best.-Nr. **978-3-14-040104-3**
Lehrerheft. Best.-Nr. **978-3-14-040105-0**

British and American Youth Culture
Von Hannspeter Bauer und Gudrun Vesper
64 S. Best.-Nr. **978-3-14-040053-4**
Lehrerheft. Best.-Nr. **978-3-14-040077-0**

Canada – More than Mounties and Lumberjacks
Von Martin Kohn
56 S. Best.-Nr. **978-3-14-040082-4**
Lehrerheft. Best.-Nr. **978-3-14-040092-3**

Globalisation – Blessing or Curse?
Von Jürgen Einhoff, Klaus Hinz und Karl Heinz Wagner
68 S. Best.-Nr. **978-3-14-040059-6**
Lehrerheft. Best.-Nr. **978-3-14-040089-3**

Hispanics in America
Von Veronika Kaiser und James Martin
72 S. Best.-Nr. **978-3-14-040044-2**
Lehrerheft. Best.-Nr. **978-3-14-040064-0**

India – Tradition and Transformation
Von Michaela Banzhaf und Alexandra Peschel
51 S. Best.-Nr. **978-3-14-040098-5**
Lehrerheft. Best.-Nr. **978-3-14-040099-2**

Ireland – Changes and Challenges
Von Maria Eisenmann
55 S. Best.-Nr. **978-3-14-040110-4**
Lehrerheft. Best.-Nr. **978-3-14-040111-1**

Our Environment – A State of Emergency?
Von Stephen Speight
59 S. Best.-Nr. **978-3-14-040108-1**
Lehrerheft. Best.-Nr. **978-3-14-040109-8**

The American Dream – Inventing a Nation
Von Hanspeter Bauer
74 S. Best.-Nr. **978-3-14-040086-2**
Lehrerheft. Best.-Nr. **978-3-14-040087-9**

The American South
Von Jürgen Einhoff und Katharina Einhoff
72 S. Best.-Nr. **978-3-14-040052-7**
Lehrerheft. Best.-Nr. **978-3-14-040076-3**

The Different Faces of Britain
Von Stephen Speight
64 S. Best.-Nr. **978-3-14-040085-5**
Lehrerheft. Best.-Nr. **978-3-14-040095-4**

The Fascination and Risks of Technology
Von Stephen Speight
56 S. Best.-Nr. **978-3-14-040055-8**
Lehrerheft. Best.-Nr. **978-3-14-040079-4**

The Mass Media – From Gutenberg to Gates
Von Stephen Speight und Karsten Witsch
64 S. Best.-Nr. **978-3-14-040088-6**
Lehrerheft. Best.-Nr. **978-3-14-040096-1**

William Shakespeare: A Midsummer Night's Dream
Von Rainer Gocke und Angela Stock
104 S. Best.-Nr. **978-3-14-040058-9**
Lehrerheft. Best.-Nr. **978-3-14-040068-8**

William Shakespeare: Macbeth
Von Rainer Gocke und Angela Stock
136 S. Best.-Nr. **978-3-14-040041-1**
Lehrerheft. Best.-Nr. **978-3-14-040061-9**

William Shakespeare: Much Ado About Nothing
Von Rainer Gocke und Franziska Quabeck
110 S. Best.-Nr. **978-3-14-040118-0**
Lehrerheft. Best.-Nr. **978-3-14-040119-7**

William Shakespeare: Othello
Von Anke Weber
147 S. Best.-Nr. **978-3-14-040069-5**
Lehrerheft. Best.-Nr. **978-3-14-040102-9**

William Shakespeare: Romeo and Juliet
Von Norbert Timm
143 S. Best.-Nr. **978-3-14-040056-5**
Lehrerheft. Best.-Nr. **978-3-14-040081-7**

William Shakespeare: The Sonnets
Von Anke Weber
48 S. Best.-Nr. **978-3-14-040114-2**
Lehrerheft. Best.-Nr. **978-3-14-040115-9**

William Shakespeare: Bits From The Bard
Nach Themenschwerpunkten zusammengestellt
Von Norbert Timm
48 S. Best.-Nr. **978-3-14-040057-2**
Lehrerheft. Best.-Nr. **978-3-14-040097-8**

Weitere Titel sind in Vorbereitung.